THE WORLD OF

D0760401

A series of uniform paperback editions
reprinting some of the most popular and
readable narratives from the world of
the cruising – and racing – sailor, past
and present.

1 Close-Hauled   K. Adlard Coles
2 When the Crew Matter Most   Erroll Bruce
3 Terschelling Sands   Frank Mulville

I cannot see what others see;
Wisdom alone is kind to me,
Wisdom that comes from Agony.

*   *   *

Wisdom that lives in the pure skies,
The untouched star, the spirit's eyes:
O Beauty, touch me, make me wise,

MASEFIELD

FRANK MULVILLE

TERSCHELLING
SANDS

© Frank Mulville 1968

First published in Great Britain 1968 by Herbert Jenkins Ltd

First published in paperback in Great Britain by
Nautical Books
An imprint of Conway Maritime Press Ltd
24 Bride Lane, Fleet Street
London EC4Y 8DR

ISBN 0 85177 422 9

Also by Frank Mulville

In Granma's Wake: *Girl Stella*'s Voyage to Cuba
Rustler on the Beach
Schooner *Integrity*
Single-Handed Cruising and Sailing

Printed in Great Britain

Foreword

When *Transcur's* keel ground into the Terschelling Sand it made an impression on my mind which has never left it. For a seaman to run his vessel aground was then, as it is now, the ultimate folly. Twenty years ago, when cruising foreign in small boats was a less usual pastime than today, the way out of folly usually lay only within your own resources. There was no VHF radio and *Transcur* hǎd no echo sounder; the coastguard service was patchy in comparison to now and the inshore waters of Holland as of England were comparatively deserted. I came to believe, after much heart-searching, that I made the right decision in sending Celia, Anne and the two boys off in the life raft. At the time and for years afterwards I was consumed by doubts. I discovered later what I must have sensed at the time, that I operate more effectively in an emergency when I am by myself. The experience on the Terschelling Sands gave me my first real experience of solitude in the ocean. I never forgot it.

Two years later I suffered another grounding, with almost the same crew on board, in which the ketch *Girl Stella* was wrecked in Flores in the Azores. It was after this experience that I began to sail alone, retracing *Girl Stella's* passage from England to Cuba, single-handed this time, in the boat I still have, the gaff-rigged cutter *Iskra*.

Since then I have become much attached to *Iskra* – she has worked her way into my affections in the same way as *Transcur* did through adventures, shared experiences and the day to day business of living with a boat. Apart from the Cuba voyage, in which I was a learner in the business of single-handed sailing, *Iskra* has taken me to the Bahamas, to the eastern seaboard of America from Long Island to Nova Scotia, to Norway, Scotland, Denmark and recently to Iceland. All this experience stems directly from the Terschelling Sand, where I first conceived the notion that I wanted to sail single-handed.

These single-handed capers and the advance of time have brought me full circle in my attitudes towards sailing and the sea. I no longer crave solitude and have lost the belief that I can do it all better by myself. I prefer to share the pleasure and the anguish of sailing with others which, after all, was what persuaded me to take my family sailing to Terschelling.

Frank Mulville
1987

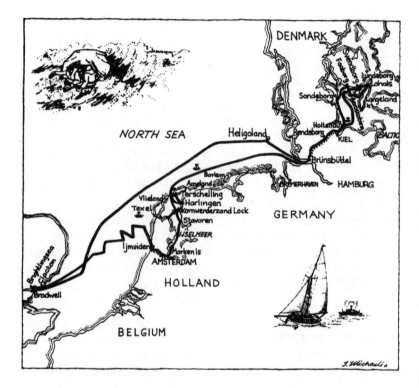

DENMARK

NORTH SEA

Heligoland

Sonderborg

Holtenau
Rendsborg

KIEL

BALTIC

Brünsbüttel

BREMERHAVEN HAMBURG

Borkum
Amelandं
Terschelling
Vlieland
Texel
Harlingen
Komwerderzand Lock
Stavoren

IJSELMEER

GERMANY

Ijmuiden

Marken Is

AMSTERDAM

HOLLAND

Brightlingsea
Clacton

Bradwell

BELGIUM

J. Michaelis

Chapter One

From Bradwell to the coast of Denmark is the best part of 350 miles across the boisterous North Sea. Although we would never venture to think of the North Sea with any feeling but the deepest respect, Celia and I were confident and easy in our minds about crossing it in *Transcur*. We had been through the Bay of Biscay in this same faithful boat three years previously with the same crew and we felt, not without reason, that we could match anything we were likely to meet in the North Sea with experiences already encountered in the Bay. If it blew as hard, surely the seas would not be as steep and dangerous as they had been a hundred miles south of Ushant. There, the sea bed falls away precipitously from 80 fathoms to 2,000 fathoms in the space of ten miles, causing the turbulence which strikes fear into the stomachs of ladies travelling by the P. & O. and gives to the Bay its notoriety. The North Sea on the other hand has an even and much shallower bed and the seas, although they can be steep, run more true and are less confused. Good harbours that a yacht can run into are available along the Dutch and German seaboards if the going should get too tough for our meagre resources of stamina and strength—difficult harbours perhaps but well marked and safe. Finally, the prevailing wind blows from between south-west and north-west and this should take us to Denmark without too great difficulty. As for the journey back—well, that could look after itself when the time came. If we worried too much about our return we would never leave the sanctuary of the English coast. "We've never ever worried about getting back before", Celia said as we studied the chart, "so I don't see that there's much point in starting now".

As we slipped quietly through Bradwell Creek on the ebb tide a light westerly breeze came ruffling across the Blackwater to cool the hot sun and to hasten us on our way. We hoisted the mainsail, the foresail and the big headsail and bore away towards the Bench Head, the Wallett, the Sunk and the open North Sea. Anne and Celia were busy stowing the last of the stores while Patrick and I went carefully round the decks coiling down and stowing away harbour gear and lashing down dinghy oars, mop, boat hook and anything else that might come loose if the weather should take a blustery turn. Adrian was in the cabin absorbed in hoisting his bear up to one of the port-hole handles and then, with a system of ropes and pulleys which he had devised, moving the bear on to the lavatory seat in the fo'c'sle. It was an apparently satisfying and absorbing pastime. The pale green shores of the familiar Blackwater slipped past as *Transcur* sailed herself easily, a line round the tiller, in a calm sea and a fair wind and tide.

Transcur is an Essex fishing smack built some time at the turn of the century. Mr. Shuttleworth in Paglesham has known her all his life and maintains that she was built, together with another *Transcur* in 1895 at Aldous's Yard in Brightlingsea. "There was the big Transcur and the little Transcur" he told us "and yours is the little 'un. My grandfather knew her well." According to the Customs House in Colchester she was first registered for fishing in 1910 and her number was CK 365 but this does not mean that she was only built in that year. She is much changed since those days and her long bowsprit, 12 ft. of it out over the stem, is all that remains of her smack's rig. The previous owner altered her rig from the old traditional gaff of a smack to Bermudian. The new mast which he put in fits her nicely and she sails well and is probably more handy than she had been. It was because he found it hard work to hoist the old gaff sail with its heavy gear that he had her converted, but Celia and I think it a lasting shame that it was found necessary to alter her rig so completely. She could have been made easier to handle and still have kept the gaff rig with all its advantages.

A heavy displacement boat like *Transcur* cannot be driven with nothing but her conventional headsails and the slim Bermudian mainsail. There is not enough power to shift her through the water—particularly with the wind aft—in anything less than a force six breeze. When we first owned her she used to wallow and flop in a light breeze like a blowzy old woman. To overcome this trouble we designed for her a terylene headsail of enormous size, hoisting from the bowsprit-end to the top of the mast with the clew abaft the shrouds. This sail, of light weight but very strong material, is bigger than the mainsail itself and when it is set it makes up for the extra mainsail that *Transcur* ought to have, with the added advantage of giving her better balance. But boats, like most things in life, are the product of compromise; if you go to an extreme one way you pay for it in another. We pay for our big sail in the difficulty of handling it and in the strain it puts on all our gear, which was never designed to carry it. The big headsail, with a stiff breeze in it, is a fierce, ill-mannered, almost uncontrollable animal of prodigious strength. It can pick a man off the deck bodily, hurl him into the scuppers and then go on to shake and shiver until every nail and timber and spar in the boat is quivering like the bones of a neurotic skeleton. When we first had it, every cleat and stanchion in the boat was wrenched from its fastenings, fingers and arms were bruised, iron blocks were broken in half, halliards were parted and swear words were invented in its honour that would make a tug skipper blush. Now we have learnt how to control it, provided that nothing goes wrong when it is set. The strength of the sail can be controlled only by art and now Patrick and I can set it and get it in without too much wear and tear on fingers and tempers. Patrick understands the sail, is conscious of its great power and for all that he is only eight years old, he is more use to me in setting it than most men with ten times his strength. All the same, the big headsail is our bête-noire

9

—sometimes it gets us into trouble and sometimes, if we are already in trouble, it can make an uncomfortable situation into a dangerous one.

Apart from the big headsail *Transcur* is straightforward and conventional on deck. She has a built up cabin top which was constructed when she was converted from a smack to a yacht in 1925. The then owner made the conversion sensibly and with due regard to the boat's looks as well as her handiness. He left wide side decks and the old smack's bulwarks so that you can walk round the decks even in rough weather with a sense of being in her instead of on her, as is the case with most modern boats. The dinghy fits exactly in its place upside down over the fore hatch leaving room to get for'ard of it to handle the anchor chain or abaft it to the halliards which are made fast to the mast and to a pin rail. She has two skylights in the cabin top which light the saloon and the galley. They leak, like all skylights, so that we now have covers for them with polythene windows sewn into the material, which keep out the water and let in light. Unlike any other smack conversion I have seen, she has a deep cockpit, large enough to seat four in comfort but not so big as to take up too much valuable space. The 25 gallon tanks for water and petrol are under the cockpit seats on either side and abaft the cockpit there is a space under the counter for stowing ropes, spare anchors, water cans and a small sea anchor which we have never used in anger. The emergency life raft stows across the after deck under the tiller.

One day in the winter Celia had said "What would we do if we really got into trouble?" "I suppose we would try to launch the dinghy—but if it was rough. . . ." We both know that our dinghy is useless in anything but a flat calm in harbour. Even then it will only take all of us, including Anne, if we all sit stock still and are all perfectly sober. Its freeboard is then one inch. "I suppose if Transcur were sinking we would just have to go." "You mean jump overboard in life jackets?" Celia asked. "Well, yes, I suppose so." Then there were some persistent questions. "How long would we last in a rough sea with the children? Suppose no one picked us up for a day . . . or all night? Suppose we hit a rock, or a sandbank and Transcur broke up? Suppose she sprung a leak and began to sink?"

The life raft arrived in a yellow box like a medium sized but very heavy suitcase. There was a space under *Transcur*'s tiller, between the after cockpit coaming and the rudder post, which might have been made for it and was stowed there, unobtrusive yet ready in an instant. It was the only space on deck which was not already in use. A length of rather flimsy looking nylon cord like a loose entrail grew out of its side and the instructions told us that if you threw the suitcase overboard and pulled sharply on this cord, a full sized life raft would materialise. It was, they said, big enough for four people who would be quite safe inside in the roughest sea, protected from the weather by a canopy which fastened all round, and kept warm by the heat from their own bodies. Patrick and Adrian were excited when it arrived, "It would be smashing fun to go in it" Adrian said "Can we try it now?" "Certainly not." Once the string has been pulled and the compressed gas released the raft cannot be folded back into its suitcase again except by the manufacturer. Celia looked at it sceptically "I suppose it does what it says it will do" she said. "Anyway the fact that it's there makes me feel better. It's the least one can do." "I don't imagine we shall ever use it in anger" I replied, "It was very expensive but at least it doesn't take up much space. I suppose it might be useful for rescuing other people." It had never entered our heads that anything could ever happen to *Transcur*. She always seemed so large and solid and safe that we were used to thinking of her as being beyond destruction.

The children regarded *Transcur* as their second home; indeed, to Patrick in the summer she is his first home and our house is his second. Adrian has never showed such single-minded enthusiasm for the boat as Patrick, but he as well accepts her as part of his life. We have owned her since Patrick was six months old and he came boating with us in his carry-cot. When Adrian was that age we took him to the Channel Islands and to Brittany, although he never went ashore from the beginning to the end of the cruise. He would lie for hours on end in his cot on the cabin top, playing with a loose reef point which dangled from the sail above his head. Three years later we took them across the Bay of Biscay to Spain, so that they are both veterans of several long sea passages in *Transcur* and, generally speaking, they behave like veterans—taking the extremes of pleasure and discomfort in their strides. For boating is a business of extremes. The pleasure and beauty that sometimes come our way is breathtaking in its intensity and there is a deep rewarding sense of achievement which is unique. Equally, the discomforts and dangers are often harassing, frightening, frustrating and disheartening.

Anne is our crew. She does not know a great deal about boats, nor does she pretend to, but she has qualities that we lack and which we would be hard put to find in any other crew whether a man or a woman. She actually likes cooking and shopping for food, particularly in foreign parts. If we had another man with us instead of Anne, Celia's life would be little more than domestic drudgery—a round of providing food and looking after children. But Anne takes pleasure in relieving Celia of much of this work, freeing her to take part in sailing and navigating the boat which is what she likes best. The children love Anne and appreciate her firm yet sympathetic hand. When she is not sailing with us, Anne is the Matron of a big London hospital where her authority goes without question. With us the awful presence is tempered with kindness, humour and a desire to fit in with our sometimes eccentric ways. But when roused or overteased, she can be formidable and we know that she has only to rattle her starched cuffs to strike us with terror. She can steer a good course and I always sleep sound in the knowledge that *Transcur* will not veer half a point when she is at the helm. Above all she has logic, unlike Celia or I, and her clear mind leads her straight to obvious solutions while Celia and I flounder.

The wind freshened a little as we sailed through the Wallett and out towards the Sunk light vessel. We had tea as Clacton pier slipped past and when the boys' bedtime came the big crane on Felixstowe dock was behind us and fast disappearing into the haze at the end of a most lovely day. We all clustered

12

round the chart as I laid off the course from the Outer Gabbard light vessel to the Texel, off the north coast of Holland. We were full of optimism and ambitious calculations. "If the wind keeps steady we should be up to Texel by to-morrow night" I said, "and then we'll bear away a point and head for Lim Fiord", I took out the large scale chart, "up here, near the top of Denmark." "It looks like a lovely place" Anne said, pointing to the chain of lakes and narrow passages which connect the North Sea to the Kattegat. Patrick and Adrian were forced reluctantly into their pyjamas and came out into the cockpit for a last look at the ebbing day. Then they were tucked into their bunks and visited by each of us for a last good night. Celia mixed a drink and she and Anne and I sat in the cockpit watching the slender finger of light from the Outer Gabbard swing relentlessly round the horizon. "To Denmark" Anne said "To Denmark . . . to Denmark." Just then the wind fell light.

The wind, that had pulled *Transcur* over such a brave day's run, had given us such a fine send off for our passage and had lifted up our hopes of a rapid trip across the North Sea and a fast fair journey, petered out to a gentle breeze and in a few more moments to a flat calm. The sombre moon heaved itself out of the sea and set the surface of the water glistening and sparkling. It reflected the soft light from *Transcur*'s white sails now hanging lifeless and inert. The beauty of the night stunned us into silence. Celia got us another drink and we sat quietly waiting for the breeze to come back, but there was no sign in the sky that there would ever be wind again, no cloud, no ripple on the sea, no sound, no movement. I said "Let's have supper, maybe there'll be a breeze later on." It had never entered my head that we should be becalmed. I was mentally prepared for rollicking stiff breezes, watches spent in exhilarating combat with the straining tiller, stinging spray flying into my face when I turned towards the wind. Instead, everything was slack and lifeless. After supper Celia said "Perhaps we should start the engine—then maybe the breeze will come back." At ten o'clock we set watches, first myself, then Anne, then Celia, and began to use the motor. *Transcur* gathered way again under power, rolling gently in the long swell

13

so that the boom swung rhythmically from side to side. Celia and Anne went to sleep.

The engine ran without a flutter of complaint. It had to be stopped every two hours to check the level of the oil and to screw down the grease nipples on the water pump and on the stern gland. It began to smell a little when it got really hot and a light haze of leaking exhaust fumes rose from it to escape out of the open skylight in the alley-way. The engine is on the starboard side of the space we call the alley-way which leads from the cockpit into *Transcur*'s main cabin. The propeller shaft goes out through the starboard quarter so that the engine tends to push *Transcur* in a circle to port, a tendency that has to be allowed for when steering under the engine. Being right inside and not exposed to damp and drips under the cockpit floor, the engine is always dry and is protected from all weather. Having the shaft through the quarter means that there is no wood cut away from the rudder to accommodate the propeller and therefore no drop in the rudder's efficiency. On the other hand our engine can only be used in calm weather or when sailing on the port tack. On the starboard tack, if the boat is heeling over, the propeller is sometimes lifted clear of the water so that it races like an airscrew and almost shakes the engine off its mountings. Its only purpose is for taking us in and out of crowded harbours or to be used at sea in a flat calm and I had never thought of it as a means of taking *Transcur* on a long passage; we carry enough petrol for a maximum of 20 hours motoring. It ran now without hesitation, rather to my surprise, because I cannot easily bring myself to trust it.

I stayed in the cockpit steering until far into the night, watching the blaze of the stars and the moon making its dignified way across the sky, hoping to catch a hint of a breeze so that I could stop the engine and settle *Transcur* to sail the course as she was intended to do. There is a special quality about the first night of a passage. For the first time you are alone and can look about you in calm anticipation. All the hurry and anxiety of getting ready is over and for better or for worse we are on our way. For weeks we have done nothing but make lists of things to be

14

bought and jobs to be done on the boat. Now the things that are forgotten and unbought will have to be done without and we must console ourselves with everything that we have remembered. At two in the morning I decided to call Celia instead of Anne as had been previously arranged, because I knew that Anne was tired to exhaustion after a busy week preparing to leave her responsibilities for a long holiday. I knew that we were all tired out and in need of a break from work and I wondered if it had been sensible to have come straight to sea on the first day of our holiday. Ideally, we should have taken the trip in easy stages. It would be several days before we were accustomed to the odd hours, the lack of sleep and the living in cramped conditions. Setting out on a long trip without a shake-down period first to get the crew well used to sea routine, and to iron out defects in the boat, is a mistake that is often made by small boat expeditions—usually with disastrous consequences.

Before calling Celia I stopped the engine to check the oil level. The silence was intense as soon as the engine's rhythm was quiet. I could hear Celia and Anne's breathing in the cabin and Adrian turned over in his bunk with a low grunt. Outside, the night was still and now that the boat's progress had stopped there was not a flicker of wind; I could see the burgee limp in the moonlight. Suddenly there was a rustle and a patter from inside the cabin and Patrick appeared in the cockpit. "Hello Daddy" he whispered sleepily, "How're we getting on?" "There's no wind, we're not getting on at all." "Why don't you run the engine?" "I am. I've stopped it to check the oil." "Will we be in Denmark to-morrow?" "No we won't. Or the next day, or the next." "Will there be a Viking ship in Denmark?" "I hope so." And then, with a non-sequitur "Will the moon ever turn round so that we can see the other side of it?" I took him to the fo'c'sle and firmly tucked him up in his bunk again. On my way back to the cockpit I touched Celia on the shoulder and she got up at once and came aft. We made a cup of tea and she settled down at the helm while I started the engine again. "This isn't much good," she said, "I hope a breeze comes in the morning." I left her sitting in the moonlight intently watching the compass, and lay down in my

15

bunk to sleep fitfully between half-conscious dreams of horrors and disasters. I dreamed that we had been in the North Sea for days without wind and without hope and that we had been carried by some inexorable current into shoal water where great rocks loomed out of the moonlight and slid past within feet of *Transcur*'s side. Then the moon died away into purple sky and the rocks themselves took on their own luminosity, *Transcur* gliding silently among them swerving from side to side like a drunk, scraping over their ragged edges. I sat up with a start to see Celia standing over me, "Are you all right? You've been hurling yourself about in your bunk like a madman. You'd better come up. It's nearly light and I think there's a breeze."

Celia was right, there was wind, a light breeze from the northwest. We stopped the engine, let go the topping lift and hoisted the big headsail and the foresail. There was enough wind to give *Transcur* about two knots and there were a few clouds to windward which held a faint promise of more. The sea had turned grey with the approaching dawn and the moon was sinking into the west. *Transcur* was covered in silver beads of dew as if she had been perspiring with the effort of running her engine through the night. Soon we saw the upper limb of the sun creep stealthily over the hard line of the horizon and suddenly it was another day. The wind freshened just a little, our speed increased and the log began to turn; we forgot that we were tired. The daylight soon woke Patrick and he came aft to inquire after our progress and to know every detail of the night's happenings. Then Adrian came bounding out of his cabin full of refreshed life and together they started to make tea. Anne emerged sleepily from her bag. "You've left me to sleep the whole night" she said reproachfully, "How are we getting on?" "Much better, we're going slowly but at least in the right direction." It was pleasant enough sailing along in the early morning sunshine although there was not quite sufficient wind for *Transcur* to sail herself with a line round the tiller. Like all heavy displacement boats she is lifeless in a light breeze and it is not until the wind increases to force three or four that she becomes, all of a sudden, awake and alive. Below force three she won't stay untended for long but falls off the wind

16

if she is left to herself for more than a few minutes. Modern light displacement boats leave her standing in these conditions. Celia and Anne laid breakfast on the big table in the cabin.

Transcur is big enough to be comfortable for us to live on board for weeks on end, without being so big that she needs a large crew to handle her. Besides Celia and Anne and I and the two children we have space for another adult but the moment the sixth person comes on board the boat becomes cramped and uncomfortable. If a boat is too small for its crew a long cruise is doomed to failure before it starts. Tempers become shorter in direct proportion to a boat's water-line length. Big heavy boats are easier to handle with a small crew than small light ones. Everything happens at a more leisurely pace and, provided the gear is sensibly designed, there should be no single job on board that one man is not able to do by himself. What limits the size of boat that you can handle by yourself is the weight of the anchor and chain. When I become so old and weak that I can no longer hoist the anchor on board by myself in a strong wind, it will be time to buy a smaller boat. But larger boats are faster and easier to sail. We have adapted *Transcur*'s accommodation so that each of the children has a commodious space to himself. Adrian's cabin is where the lavatory used to be when we bought *Transcur*—a splendid monument to the Victorian ideal of sanitation it had been. With its pipes and valves and snorting pumps it was more like the torpedo compartment of a submarine. We had unbolted it from its mounting, abstracted the tortuously bent pipes, blocked up the holes in the hull for the inlet and the outlets, and given the lavatory to a friend who installed it with great pride in a boat called *The Mary*. As far as I know it is still busy in the inner harbour at Ramsgate. "We'll have to manage without a lavatory", I said to Celia, "until we can save enough money to buy a smaller one and think of a way of stowing it". After we had had *Transcur* for a year we did buy a small lavatory and found space for it in the fo'c'sle. The old lavatory vacated a fine big space behind a sliding door on *Transcur*'s port side just forward of the galley and we were able to build in a comfortable full length bunk in which Adrian will be able to expand up to

17

a length of six feet. Patrick slept there until Adrian was born and then he moved into the fo'c'sle. On the opposite side of the alley-way to Adrian's cabin is the engine, encased in a stout wooden box with a good work top which doubles as galley table and chart space. Behind the engine is another full length quarter berth. The galley itself is inside the companionway. It has a calor gas stove under which there is a bank of lockers and storage for pots and pans.

Celia and I recently made a discovery in *Transcur* which has transformed her. One day Celia said "You know we have never cleaned out the ballast and the bilges in this boat since we had her?" When I took up the cabin floor I realised for the first time that we could get at least eight inches of extra headroom in the cabin and the alley-way by dropping the cabin floor. We would have to replace the iron ballast by lead, which is much smaller for its weight, in order to get the extra space but it seemed a reasonable price to pay for eight inches of extra height. The iron pigs of ballast, some of them weighing a good three hundred-weight, had been in *Transcur* at least since 1925 when she was first converted, and probably for longer. They were embedded in an emulsion of all the filth that had found its way into the bilge during the past thirty years and they were covered with rusty slime and muck. With the aid of two strong helpers it took two days to clear the ballast out and clean the bilges, but when it was done we could see how much more room could be made in *Transcur*'s accommodation. The eight inches has made an astonishing difference to the comfort inside. Now, Celia and I, who are both tall, can stand up straight inside—at least under the skylights—and *Transcur* had become roomier and more comfortable out of all proportion to the actual amount of space saved. The new lead pigs of ballast stow neatly along the keelson instead of sprawling out over the whole of the bilge as the iron had done, and she has become more efficient as well as roomier. She is lighter in the water without any loss of stability, she is lighter on the helm and quicker in stays. Now there is a deep step down from the galley into the alley-way and instead of bending and crouching inside the boat we can walk about like civilized human beings. We have overcome one of the greatest drawbacks of all smack conversions—the lack of headroom. All that we have sacrificed is space for bilge water under the cabin floor, but as *Transcur* hardly leaks, this is unimportant; it means that if she does leak, something has to be done to stop it, or at least to pump it out, sooner; and this is no bad thing. We are well equipped with pumps. There is a powerful Vortex rotary pump as well as a small electric pump which drains out every drop of bilge water. I don't believe there exists another smack of *Transcur*'s size with full headroom inside; she was one of the few that were built with deep draft instead of the usual three foot six draft of the average Essex smack. Her main cabin is commodious with a comfortable settee berth on each side, lockers for oilskins and clothes, bookshelves and a charcoal burning stove. It is home to us and is as comfortable and friendly as home should be.

The fo'c'sle is Patrick's domain. He sleeps on a pipe-cot which folds up against the ship's side when it is not in use and he has his own hatch that he can go in and out by if he wishes, when *Transcur* is not at sea with the dinghy stowed over the hatch. Sometimes, when he is asleep and when *Transcur* is sailing hard on the port tack he seems to cling to his bunk by willpower alone. Celia often goes anxiously for'ard in bad weather and peeps through the door to see that he is all right. He lies curled up tight towards the ship's side, fast asleep and hanging on grimly with his feet and hands, his back braced against one of the rope supports of the cot. On the starboard tack he is more relaxed, pressed against the wooden lining over *Transcur*'s frames with his sleeping bag in a mound on top of him. One would not think that the noise and the motion in the fo'c'sle in heavy weather were ideal for a small boy to go to sleep in. *Transcur* picks her bow high in the air, hangs for a moment and then plunges down. When a wave breaks over her a ton of green water thunders onto the deck above Patrick's head and the whole boat shakes with the impact. It is like being in an express train which has strayed onto the track of a big dipper. He sleeps contentedly through it all, happy and relaxed; few adults can stand more than half a minute of it without feeling the urgent need to come out on deck and breathe draughts of fresh air. All the spare sails and rope and gear of every kind is stowed in the fo'c'sle. There is a sail rack opposite Patrick's bunk—Adrian can sleep there if his cabin is occupied by an adult visitor—and under it there is a bo'sun's box with spare canvas, palm and needle, wax, twine, small rope, pieces of leather for chafing gear, marlin, lamp wicks, and an endless collection of treasures. Bunches of spare blocks, shackles, thimbles, track slides, eyelets, spare sheaves and belaying pins hang from the beam shelf and jangle against each other as *Transcur* rolls and pitches—a ground bass to the endless music of the sea against the hull. The fo'c'sle is as cosy a place as any little boy could find to do his sleeping. Celia and Anne and I sleep in the saloon when we are at sea, continuously rotating through each other's bags as the watches change so that the person coming off has a warm sleeping bag to lie in. In harbour, the cabin is left to Celia and Anne, and I sleep in the quarter berth behind the engine.

The wind stayed in the north and *Transcur* sailed reasonably fast on her course while we had breakfast, but soon afterwards it began to veer and fall light again. By ten o'clock we were close hauled and by eleven we were no longer pointing on course but were heading towards the coast of Holland. The early-morning weather forecast had predicted moderate south-westerly winds. "This is a bit unfair," Anne said, "it must change soon." Celia was more sceptical. "The weather forecast can be wrong for days on end" she said, "it's happened to us often enough before." It was frustrating for the wind to have fallen light and to have headed us at the same time. Even against a good strong breeze *Transcur* cannot make good more than about three knots and in this fitful air she was more or less stationary. What progress she did make was at an angle of thirty degrees to her course and if we kept on in this direction it would eventually bring us to the coast of Holland somewhere in the vicinity of Ijmuiden. I was tired and had become ill-tempered with our poor showing. "Bloody weather forecast's wrong as often as it's right" I complained, as if the forecast itself could make a difference to our progress. It added to our frustration that the wind ought really to have been south-westerly force three to four and made the north-easterly breeze harder to bear with.

Patrick and Adrian did not mind in the least about the weather but suffered indirectly through our own shortness of temper. They played for most of the day with cars and boats in the cabin and they gossiped endlessly with whoever happened to be steering. Occasionally they erupted into bitter quarrels over some alleged injustice on the part of one or the other of them and when this happened Celia would read to them a chapter from the ubiquitous Arthur Ransome. This always had the effect of restoring peace. Celia would also cunningly produce toys and games for them which she had kept hidden to be brought out as seemed most opportune. There was always a mystery about where these toys were secreted. Patrick knew quite well that somewhere in the boat there would be a cache of toys, many of them for him, because it was his birthday within a week.

The evening weather forecast again predicted light south-westerly winds. But the wind itself, not in the least put out by this, continued to blow from the north north-east. "We'll put her about for the night" I said, "We must be getting a bit close to the Dutch coast and I'll be happier if she's on the off-shore tack." We changed to the other tack and for good measure we took in the big headsail before it got dark and set the working jib. I did not want to risk having to take in the big headsail in the night if the weather did turn nasty. The sail was not making much difference to her speed, being close hauled in such a light breeze. Celia and I studied the chart after the boys had been put to bed. I was not quite sure of our position and I knew that my D.R. calculations were likely to be very wide of the mark. Progress all day had been so slow and the course so erratic— it had continuously been adjusted to fit with any temporary breeze that came our way—that it had been impossible to keep anything but a sketchy record of distances run between alterations of course. The log had been virtually motionless, giving a few feeble revolutions every now and then and we were at the mercy of the tidal set whose rate and direction were uncertain.

"We'll keep her on this tack all night" I said, "and see what the morning brings." I put a position on the chart which was a kind of synthesis of all our guesses and estimates and this position showed us to be about mid-way between the Texel light vessel and Ijmuiden harbour.

Anne steered whilst Celia and I went below and got into our sleeping bags. I was very tired and was looking forward to four hours uninterrupted sleep. "At least we're quite safe on this tack" I said to Anne before leaving her in the cockpit, "but let me know if you run into a lot of shipping or if you get a breeze. You'll soon have the moon for company and then it will be as light as day." I was soon deeply asleep in Anne's bunk. Two and a half hours later I felt Celia's hand on my shoulder, "There's a thick fog and I can hear a ship's engine."

I was in the cockpit in seconds, dragging on my sweater and my trousers as I went, to find the fog swirling round *Transcur* so thick that I could hardly see the mast. The navigation lights made eerie pools of green and red, the colour thrown back at us by the impenetrable gloom. Overhead, the moon was a round blob of incandescence—like a giant snowball. The steady and increasing sound of a ship's engine could be heard somewhere out ahead of us. Besides the sound of the diesel engine we could hear the noise of her propeller breaking the water—she would more than likely be a big cargo ship in ballast. The noise was swelling— getting louder and nearer every second. It was calm and *Transcur* was not making more than one or perhaps two knots. Moisture clung in big silver drops along the bottom of the boom, to the rail and to the hatch top. Tiny rivulets of wet ran down the sail from somewhere above. It was like some strange new element, half air half sea. "Get out the fog horn. She's coming closer." Celia reached into the companionway and brought out our hooter. I gave a puny blast with all the breath I could command and what seemed like a totally insignificant noise floated out into the fog. "Some hopes of a steamer hearing that above the noise of his engines" Celia said. I was just going to wake Anne and tell her to get the children up when the noise suddenly changed its bearing and seemed to grow fainter. "Thank God for

22

that, he's passed ahead of us. He must have altered course." We listened to the diminishing throb with relief and Celia made hot cocoa for us. I put on her oilskin jacket to keep out the clinging damp. "I think I'll stay up for a bit" I said, "If we run into any more shipping it will mean we are further off shore than I thought we were—out in the shipping lane—and we shall have to go about to keep clear of it." "We're certainly not getting to Denmark very fast" Celia said "I don't suppose we've made five miles all night. How far is it to Lim Fiord?" she yawned. "From here? About 250."

She went down to her bunk and left me in the fog wondering whether it would not be sensible to go into Ijmuiden if no breeze came in the morning. If we did have to go to Holland, it would really be better to make our way in behind the Frisian Islands at the south of Texel, which was more or less on our way, rather than to go to Ijmuiden. But I had no large scale chart of the long and dangerous channel from the sea to Den Helder. It would be very foolish to attempt it without one and quite impossible to do so in fog. On the other hand we could go back the odd twenty miles to Ijmuiden which was an easy entrance; Celia and I had been there before. There is a radio beacon at Ijmuiden and we would have no difficulty in finding our way in with our Mini Loop. If we did that, I thought, we could go through the canals and the Zuider Zee to the north of Holland and back into the North Sea again. As the night got colder and damper and as the fog became even more impenetrable, I thought round and round the question and the tireder I got the more convinced I became that it would be sensible to go back to Ijmuiden. At 6.45 in the morning I put the wireless on very quietly so that no one would wake and listened to the shipping forecast. It was a story of light variable and easterly winds and this time the south-westerlies were not even mentioned. I saw that the glass was falling and I thought, quite unreasonably, that it might start blowing from the north-east. When Celia and the boys woke at seven I started the engine, turned *Transcur* round and headed 140 degrees—back on our tracks. It was a bad decision—one of the worst I have ever made.

23

Chapter Two

The only way to get somewhere in a sailing boat is to make up your mind that you are going and stick at it until you get there. Professional sailors in the old days always followed this quite simple rule and they usually fetched up where they wanted to be. If they were becalmed they sat it out until a breeze came and if, when the breeze did come, it turned into a full gale against them and drove them back a hundred miles they settled down patiently to make up the lost ground when the weather moderated. This is obviously the correct way to proceed; we could easily have carried on to Denmark and we should have done so. We had plenty of stores, plenty of water, we ought to have had enough rest in the fine weather, and the boys were enjoying the trip and were well contented. "Aren't we going to Denmark after all?" Patrick asked disappointedly as soon as he knew we had altered course for Ijmuiden. "Yes we are going to Denmark but we're going to Holland first" I replied shortly. Celia and Anne were disappointed too although they did not question the decision once I had made it. "I've never been to Holland anyway" Anne said and Adrian remarked "We shall see windmills in Holland."

Celia and I had been to Holland before, years previously, in *Santa Lucia*. She had been a romantic little boat, a cutter only eighteen feet long on the water line with a graceful clipper bow and a rounded counter to match it. We had come across from Bradwell to Ijmuiden much faster and more direct than on this occasion and had thankfully picked up the lighthouse on Ijmuiden pier right over our bowsprit end. We had come shooting in between the piers of the harbour entrance on the first hard gusts of a south-westerly gale which howled and rattled among the masts in the fish harbour where we had spent the night. *Santa Lucia* had been our first love. We had loved her passionately, although we had nearly lost her on that first trip to Holland. She had been crushed against the lock wall by a Dutch oil tanker in the Parksluis in Rotterdam and she had almost sunk under us. If it had not been for the captain of a British warship who had taken pity on us and shipped *Santa Lucia* back to England, lashed on the fore deck of his frigate, we would certainly have lost her. She had been our only asset and without the money we subsequently got for her we would never have been able to buy *Transcur*.

We swore we would never go cruising in Holland again after our experiences in *Santa Lucia*. In fact, it's a wonder we ever went cruising again anywhere after our experiences in *Santa Lucia*. She took us to Brittany, to Holland and across the Bay to Spain but on each trip she frightened us so much that by the end of it we had hardly any nerves left. She was a little bit tender, she had a big open cockpit giving any sea that came aboard direct access to the bilges, and she leaked relentlessly and continuously. But she was fast, comfortable within her own limitations, seaworthy enough after we learned to handle her and she had graceful flowing romantic lines. To us she was a symbol of revolt and escape. When we went to sea in her it was in defiance of every convention. We had no money, we always left behind some business enterprise which was on the brink of financial ruin and which ought to have had our constant attention, we were living in sin, and our affairs, generally, were in ruins. Invariably, when we came back from our trips everything had to be sold to pay pressing creditors and we had to borrow money and start all over again. But *Santa Lucia* was so shapely and so noble that whenever we saw her graceful lines we knew that it was all worthwhile. She was a boat that added the distinction of real quality to any anchorage she was in.

The North Sea fog persisted through the morning. The engine ran steadily and the ever strengthening signal from the radio beacon told us that we were getting closer to Ijmuiden harbour. There was still nothing but a light northerly air and Patrick and I and Adrian took in all the sails and made a neat harbour stow. Soon the fog began to thin out and the sun to penetrate through it. A line of big Dutch trawlers bound for some North Sea fishing grounds passed us going fast in the direction we had come from and presently we saw the land—a long low yellow coast of sand dunes, apparently devoid of any habitation. "It's like a desert island" Patrick remarked. At mid-day the last of the fog evaporated and we saw the town of Ijmuiden and the harbour entrance in front of us.

We motored between the piers and up the harbour towards the big locks at the entrance to the ship canal that leads from Ijmuiden to Amsterdam. The lock was closed. "We'll tie up alongside these piles" I said "and I'll walk along to the lock and see when it is going to open." Celia stood forward with our bow line. "Jump ashore when we get alongside and make fast to that post" I said. Anne stood amidships with boat hook ready to hook on to the staging and haul us in as I went below to give the engine a kick astern. Then Celia jumped on to the wooden staging. She slipped and fell. Her right leg slithered away from under her and she lost her balance. She put her hands out to grab at a wooden rail, missed, and her left leg, with all her weight behind it, scraped across the sharp barnacled edge of the staging. She lay for a moment half on the staging and half hanging over the edge, clawing for some hold on the slippery surface of the staging, and then as *Transcur* swung closer Anne and I grabbed her and dragged her back on board, sitting her down on the cabin top by the mast. She was suddenly pale and buttons of perspiration stood out on her face as she looked down at the thin red trickle which ran down her leg and into her shoe.

Anne's voice, taking charge of the situation, roused me from

a mental stupor. "I'll look after this, you make Transcur fast."
Transcur was beginning to drift away from the staging and I grabbed the boat hook and hauled her alongside, glad to be doing something and for someone else to have taken responsibility from me. Patrick and I put out lines fore and aft and a spring to stop her from surging back and forth along the staging as motor boats went past. "What's happened to Mummy?" Patrick said in a frightened voice, "She's in the cabin and there's blood all over her leg." I went below and saw that Celia was sitting on her bunk, chalk white, with her leg out in front of her across the cabin floor. Anne had a basin of water and was bathing the filth and slime of the staging off her shin and carefully placing the broken and bruised skin back in position. I poured Celia a large brandy and took one for myself.

Patrick shouted from the deck "Daddy, the lock's open." A big steamer was coming out of the canal and the signal for vessels to enter was just being hoisted. A huge floating crane in tow of a diesel tug was manœuvring to go in. "We'll go behind that chap" I said to Patrick "Come on, you and I will have to do this now." I climbed with great care onto the slippery staging, the crimson stain already mixing with water, oil and filth and turning a dull mauve, and let go our ropes. Patrick put the engine ahead and we passed slowly into the great lock. "For God's sake be careful in that lock" Celia called out weakly from the cabin : she was remembering our experience in the Parksluis. We tied up alongside the tug, being careful to keep our bowsprit clear of the lock gates. When I went below Anne had already covered Celia's shin with soothing cream and lint and was beginning to bandage it. The angry blue bruise had begun to show and it was quite clear that she was in considerable pain although she was already making light of it. "I'll sit with my leg up either here or in the cockpit, and everyone can wait on me," she said "I shall have a fine time." But besides being painful and unpleasant it was a serious accident in every way. It would be harder to handle the boat and to look after the children with Celia more or less out of commission for at least three of four days. Her left leg was already weak owing to a previous mishap

27

and now she was quite unable to put any weight on it. It would have to be rested continuously if it was to get better quickly. Holland! I thought to myself, we get nothing but bad luck in Holland. "If you like we'll pack up the whole trip and go home now before anything else dreadful happens to us in this wretched country." But Celia is not easily put off. "No, I shall be all right soon and perhaps our luck will change now. There's no need to turn back because of this."

The water began to drain out of the lock and *Transcur* descended vertically until it seemed that we were at the bottom of a well with a long blue slit of daylight far up above the mast. Our voices were flung back at us from the smooth damp walls of the lock as if we were being mocked by some imitative monster. I remembered how Celia had shrieked with terror and despair in *Santa Lucia* when the tanker had effortlessly crushed the little boat's ribs and splintered her timbers. It had been as if a giant had Celia herself between forefinger and thumb and had been slowly breaking and squeezing the life out of her. On that occasion we had received scant sympathy from the Dutch whose only concern had been the possible cost and inconvenience to themselves. Now we were at the bottom of another Dutch lock and had been overtaken by another misfortune although perhaps not so dire a one as on the previous occasion. The great gates began to swing open and I started the engine, looking anxiously round to see that no other vessel was near enough to cause us any damage before Patrick put the engine ahead and we slipped safely out into the North Sea canal. We need have had no fear because normally the Dutch handle their canal craft with great skill and seamanlike consideration for small boats of every description. We had been unlucky in *Santa Lucia* and we know that the carelessness and impatience on the part of the Dutch skipper on that occasion was a rare exception.

Once we got clear of the lock and into the North Sea canal Celia became more cheerful and the colour came back into her face. She was installed in the cockpit where she could sit with her bandaged leg up on the locker top as we set off down the canal towards Amsterdam. Anne made lunch for us as we watched the incredibly varied life of this modern, bustling waterway. Every five minutes there was something new and utterly absorbing for the boys to look at. Great shipbuilding yards with half completed ships on the ways, a vast water-borne crane like a praying mantis lifting some strange variety of machinery high in the air, a fine Dutch ocean-going tug with a damaged ship in tow, great liners going out to sea from Amsterdam, hurrying ferries and launches and barges of every type and description. As we motored along the canal the volume and variety of traffic increased until we came up to the city of Amsterdam itself with its skyline of towers and churches dominated by the arched roof of the railway station in the centre of the town. The waterway was a confusion of ferries, barges, boats, pleasure steamers and ships hurrying in every direction so that it became impossible to pilot *Transcur* by any recognised rule of the road. We avoided collision only by using the psychological direction finding impulses that enable people in a crowded street to avoid running into one another and that allow birds to wheel and sweep in cohesion without apparent communication. We searched for the Sixhaven where we had laid in *Santa Lucia* but found it no longer there—disappointing, this, because we had enjoyed our stay in the Sixhaven ten years previously. Baron von Hoevel had looked after us well. He had allowed us to use his slip so that we could haul *Santa Lucia* out of the water for yet another of our perennial attempts to stop her from leaking. We had looked forward to renewing a charming acquaintanceship. Now, there seemed to be no place for a yacht to stop in Amsterdam and so we continued up the canal past the city in the hope of finding the locks that lead from the North Sea canal to the Iselmeere. As has happened so often before I had been caught out for lack of charts. Having left home with no intention of coming to Holland we had not provided ourselves with sailing directions and had to rely once again on the Cruising Association handbook, a publication which we tend to regard with caution but which, nonetheless, has helped us many times.

Anne saw another yacht ahead of us which seemed to be following a purposeful course through Amsterdam. "Let's follow him" she said "he must be going somewhere and wherever he brings up we can tie alongside him and look at his chart." We followed this yacht through Amsterdam until the press of traffic began to thin and we saw him go into a lock where the canal appeared to end. This lock was an altogether smaller and safer looking place than the big ship lock at Ijmuiden had been, with nothing more sinister in it than a couple of barges and three yachts. We slid through the gates and made fast alongside one of the yachts. The Dutch owner, who spoke English as most Dutchmen do, looked on us with a kind of scandalised pity when I told him that we had come to Holland more or less by mistake, unprovided with charts and completely ignorant of our whereabouts. He told us that we were in Schellingworde and that there was a little yacht club on the other side of the lock where we would be able to lie for a day. He pointed to a high level bridge and explained to us that through this was the Iselmeere.

Before the North Sea canal had been built and before the Zuider Zee had been closed in by the great sea barrage across the north of Holland, Schellingworde had been the main point of entry to Amsterdam. The Zuider Zee in those days had been a vast tidal estuary and it was the building of the great dyke to the north that had changed its character and its name. When we finally got to the other side of the lock we found the little yacht club and managed to squeeze *Transcur* stern first between two piles so that we could jump ashore onto the wooden staging.

At last the boys were able to go ashore and run off some of the energy they had been storing up inside themselves for the past three days. They raced backwards and forwards along the quay like dogs let off the chain first thing in the morning. Anne and I went ashore with them when *Transcur* was properly tied up, in a vain search for ice cream in the tiny village of Schellingworde. There was no ice cream, but there was a children's playground although no other children were to be seen, and Anne and I were able to relax on the grass in the last of the evening sunshine while the boys exhausted themselves on swings, seesaws and a climbing frame that might have been put there solely for Adrian's pleasure.

Celia was left on board to read and to rest her leg in the cabin. "This couldn't be a worse start to a cruise to Denmark" I said to Anne "We're in the wrong country, we've no charts, no money, and Celia is a cripple—my God, just have a look at that." And I pointed up to the tall trees that ringed the little park we were in, whose topmost leaves rustled and swayed with a fresh breeze that was blowing true from the west—the breeze that would at this moment have been sending us skimming along the North European Coast towards Lim Fiord. But Anne refused to be cast down.

"I don't think it's so bad" she said. "We shall have a fine time in Holland—at least I shall enjoy it. Don't forget we've only been going for three days. We've still got plenty of time to get to Denmark. And Celia's leg will be all right if only we can persuade her to rest it. Anyway, the boys will enjoy a day or so in Holland."

We agreed to set off to Amsterdam by bus on the following morning to buy charts and if possible get sailing directions for the Iselmeere and the ports along the north Dutch coast. The only problem was that we had no Dutch money for our bus fares and Schellingworde had no bank. We doubted if there was anyone willing to change money in the village. But these problems solved themselves for us very quickly. When we got back to *Transcur* we found a young Dutchman—a student from Amsterdam University—who was walking up and down the jetty admiring the boat and who greeted us in English when we came to go aboard. We soon made friends with him and he agreed to lend us a few schillings until the next day.

We got up early the next morning and when I looked out of the cabin I saw that it was now blowing very strongly from the south-west. "There you are" Celia said "we would have messed about in the North Sea until all our petrol was gone and then there would have been far more wind than is good for us. We're better off where we are." But this reasoning did not convince me in the least. I couldn't get the picture out of my mind of *Transcur* bowling along with the sheets free, a wide even wake, and pushing a curling hissing bow wave in front of her towards Denmark.

31

We took the two boys to Amsterdam by bus leaving Celia on board with instructions to rest her leg as much as possible. The bus meandered through the suburbs of Amsterdam, uninteresting in themselves but enlivened by the occasional sight of a great ship towering up above the roof tops. Soon we found ourselves opposite the railway station and a quick trip on the ferry took us across the North Sea canal again to the centre of the city. Our first job was to change money and then to sit down at a café for ice cream and coffee. Then we got hold of a tourist map and went by bus to the Water Tourist Bureau where we were able to buy small scale charts of the Iselmeere from a charming English-speaking girl. She told us how to get to the Dutch Hydrographic Office where we would be able to buy proper charts of the channels from the north of the Iselmeere out into the North Sea. More buses took us through the city once again, to the dock area where we made our way through a maze of alleys and canal bridges to the fine modern chart depot. The officer in charge of the depot helped us pick the charts we would need and made us wait while the latest small corrections were made. He was quite insistent on this point. "You must not take the charts until they are corrected right up to date" he said. The boys were now exhausted by the new impressions they had been absorbing and by the high speed walking and travelling on buses. We had lunch at a small café by the side of the harbour and this revived our spirits. "Now I feel better" I said to Anne, "We've got charts and we've got money and provided Celia's leg gets better we should be able to pass quickly through Holland and start on our passage again." "Don't be in too much of a hurry" Anne said, "I'm beginning to enjoy this country."

Chabter Three

The next day was bright and sunny and the strong westerly wind eased in the afternoon when we decided to leave and make our way up the Iselmeere. The boys had consumed a good ration of Amsterdam ice cream and having been ashore for most of the day they were more than ready to start off again. There were signs that Celia's leg was beginning to get better, although it was still painful to her, but by resting it as much as she could she thought she had got over the worst. We paid our debt to the young student who had kindly loaned us money, slipped our lines and sailed out of the little yacht basin. There was a road bridge across our path but we had found out, or thought we had, that the bridge would open at five in the evening. We set our sails and made our way towards the swinging sector in the centre of it but it showed no sign that it would open and however close we sailed to it and however fiercely we blew our hooter the solid Dutchman sitting in the control house continued immersed in his newspaper without taking the slightest notice of us. At six, A Dutch coaster came out of the lock from the North Sea canal and steamed steadily towards the bridge. The man in the control house at once stopped the traffic and began to raise it. The coaster went through first, then an old ketch and we followed, just in time before the arms of the bridge began to fall back into place.

With our Dutch tourists' chart we were able to pick up the channel buoys quite easily. The shores of the Iselmeere were flat and featureless, as you would expect in Holland and we identified towers of churches and of stadthuises that were miles inland. Out on our starboard side we could see the derricks and cranes of yet another great dyke under construction whereby a further tract of Dutch soil would be reclaimed from the water. The country that we could see seemed to be a thickly populated and friendly place, with farmhouses close together, their roofs and chimneys showing over the dyke. The farms seemed to be quite small so that you would not have to travel more than a quarter of a mile between one and the next. Fat cattle gazed sombrely at us from the tops of the dykes. The wind was now light but *Transcur* made reasonable progress across the smooth water with her big headsail set, so that soon we began to leave the old ketch far astern—certainly by the looks of her she would be no racer. The evening was fine and the boys towed their boats over the stern, an occupation which they seldom tire of, while Celia sat in the cockpit with her foot up and steered. The boys' boats are specially designed for towing over the stern. They are flat pieces of board with bluff flared bows so that the boats trail like speedboats and leap from wave to wave in a pleasing manner. The upper works are made from any old pieces of wood that can be found on board, a nail serves as a mast and the boys rig them with pieces of twine and bunting. We discovered early on that they usually like toys that are improvised out of old bits and pieces much better than expensive articles bought in shops.

Sailing on a huge artificial lake was a new experience to us and *Transcur* seemed slightly out of her element. The Iselmeere, before it became a lake, was the Zuider Zee; the great dyke across the northern entrance to it was finally closed in 1932. It offers a fine cruising ground to hundreds of yachts, Dutch, English, French, and German and it is a superb stretch of water for anyone who likes sailing under these conditions. The old towns of the Zuider Zee are still there and although their character is much changed they are still picturesque and very charming. You can go through the canal at Stavoren into an extensive system of lovely inland lakes where it is possible to spend a very excellent holiday. All that was wrong with it for us, at least for myself, was that we had come there more or less by accident and we did not really wish to tarry a minute longer than was necessary. *Transcur* seemed to slap the little waves with her bow as if she was frustrated of the long easy motion at sea. In fact she is not a very suitable boat for sailing in inland waterways—light displacement sloops are best suited to the close quarters of canals and tiny harbours. *Transcur*'s long bowsprit strikes terror into the hearts of modern yachtsmen—particularly Continental yachtsmen who are not used to such things—and they cower down in their cockpits as it sweeps round like a flail when she comes into a crowded berth. We are quite used to the bowsprit and regard it affectionately and quite naturally as part of the boat but I have noticed that other yacht owners are hostile towards it. German yachts, we found, were particularly frightened of it. The traditional Dutch boyer is probably still the boat which is best suited to these waters. They are surprisingly fast, very roomy and comfortable inside and have the immense advantage of shallow draught and the ability to take the ground. Above all, they are attractive to look at and seem to suit the rather baroque scenery, whereas *Transcur* is quite out of place with her coarser North Sea lines.

The boys went to bed earlier than usual—they were tired after the long trek to Amsterdam—and as the sun was setting we rounded the lighthouse on the point of Marken Island. We had some difficulty in finding the entrance as our tourist chart was confusing and slightly inaccurate but in the last of the dusk we passed into a miniature harbour between red and green lighthouses and tied up in Marken village. "Perhaps there will be some gay life here" I said to Anne "We'll go ashore and see what we can find. Dancing girls, and people thumping the table with beer mugs is what I want." But the village of Marken was quaint and quiet with serious looking men hurrying along the narrow streets and life soberly confined behind heavy lace

35

curtains. We found a café which was sleepily open and we drank there until the proprietor succeeded in yawning us out of the door. *Transcur* lay snug and comfortable alongside the quay in the centre of the town and we consoled ourselves with cups of cocoa. "So much for the gay life" Anne said and catching the mood of the place we went to bed.

The next morning we saw the reason for Marken's existence. The tripper boats began to arrive in a steady stream at ten o'clock so that by lunch time there were hundreds of German, French and even a few English visitors darting about the island like startled cockroaches. We soon had to shift our berth so that we would not be photographed to death and we found a measure of peace on the outer wall of the harbour. The local inhabitants appeared from their houses dressed to a man in national costume and soon every house let down its front shutters, converting its windows into counters quite covered with souvenirs. A tall lively Dutchman came along the quay to visit us. "Your boat looks to me like a British fisherman" he said and we invited him on board for an English gin which he valued highly. He had been at sea during the war and had spent some time in English merchant ships.

"There was none of this when I was a boy" he said pointing to the tourists on the quay "In those days we used to work for our living." Marken had once put a fine fishing fleet to sea, he told us. In those days every man in the town would go fishing in the Zuider Zee and further afield. The boats would all go out on Monday morning and would not come back until Saturday, leaving only women, children and old people in Marken. The town had several times been destroyed by fire and inundated by floods and each time this happened the patient, industrious Markenaars had rebuilt the traditional wooden houses in the old style. The island had been remote and the people had developed their own habits of life in complete independence. Now, for the benefit of tourists, the women still wore the costume peculiar to Marken, some of the magnificent lace dresses were handed down from mother to daughter for generations. The lace-work is of a peculiarly rare design made only in Marken. But now the people

36

are more interested in selling souvenirs to tourists. "It's easier to get rich that way and it's not such hard work as fishing". He told us how the dykes had been constructed and how the land had been drained and reclaimed, first being sown with a special kind of fern to bind together the soil, then with root crops and finally with grass and corn. Soon, he said, most of the Iselmeere would be reclaimed and then Holland would have more land to house its increasing population. In spite of the tourists he could not deny that the Dutch were still a tremendously industrious people. "God made the world" he quoted "but the Dutch made Holland."

Patrick and Adrian played in the dinghy, rowing and sculling round the harbour and making boats and submarines out of old pieces of wood. Celia went shopping in the village to try out her leg, which was much better, and came back having had the greatest difficulty in buying anything that did not have the Dutch equivalent of "A present from Marken" written on it. She bought bread and milk after much effort but failed on tomatoes and potatoes. Anne hauled me to the top of the mast in a bo'sun's chair from where the view of the countryside was superb. We rove off a new set of flag halyards as the old ones had broken while *Transcur* had been rolling and pitching in the North Sea. By lunch time we were sick of Marken and decided to leave as soon as possible. We sailed out into the Iselmeere again where the wind was north-westerly. But as the day passed it gradually headed us so that it was already late in the afternoon by the time we had covered the seventeen miles to Enkhuizen. We passed close to the town but decided, as it did not look enticing, that we would go on either for Stavoren or for Medemblik depending on what the wind finally decided to do. We tacked close on and off shore for an hour or so, working our way along the coast past the tall towers of Osterdijk and Andijk and then the wind went into the north north-west. We made a course right across the Iselmeere for Stavoren as it freshened. It got dark and misty but we didn't mind because we were sure of our position and Stavoren was nicely tucked under our lee. Soon Anne spotted the lights of the harbour entrance and we swept in, gybing into the inner harbour and bringing up with our sails flapping and banging alongside a small, rich German yacht. The owner let out a cry of alarm when he saw *Transcur* looming at him through the dark and realised that we proposed to tie alongside him. Anne threw him our lines as I let the sails down and we breasted in against his immaculate white fender.

"Surely here there will be gaiety and singing and dancing" I said to Anne, "All these yachtsmen must be revelling in some great drinking party. There'll be dancing girls, strip-tease and lots of Old Geneva. We'll be back by dawn" I said to Celia "probably roaring and shouting and singing bawdy songs."

It was ten o'clock when Anne and I went ashore across the decks of a dozen silent, deserted yachts. We walked along the quay towards the town and searched the quiet streets for some sign of life. We found a dimly lit hotel and penetrated an inner lounge where two groups of men sat in silence munching cheese biscuits. The barman dozed on his high stool immobile and silent like a statue. We rattled on the counter and he opened a lazy eye and served us beer. "Where's the night life? The dancing? Jive?" He glanced at the clock "In Stavoren" he said in English, "everyone is asleep." He eyed us sympathetically "English?", we nodded. "This is Holland where the people are sober and hard-working. At night they go to bed and early in the morning they get up and start work". But things were not always so quiet in Stavoren which was once one of the great towns of the North European seaboard. In ancient times the town was surrounded by a great wall and was the capital and royal residence of Friesland. In those times the Zuider Zee itself did not exist and it was possible to walk right across from Stavoren to Enkhuizen. A series of great floods in the fourteenth century created the Zuider Zee and this, combined with disastrous reverses in war reduced the great city of Stavoren to nothing more than a village.

The next day we moved along the quay and lay astern of a fine old Dutch fishing boat, now used as a yacht, with the owner and his son and daughter on board. The girl was beautiful, with fine features and her hair tied behind her head and hanging down her back. She was tall and elegant and lent grace to the whole harbour—a beautiful girl is a rare enough sight in Holland where features are coarse. Even the gloomy German whom we had laid alongside in the night, brightened as he walked along the quay and saw her sitting on the old fishing boat's main hatch.

We walked into the town, changed some more money and Celia and Anne began to re-stock our store cupboards for the next part of the passage, which would be a long leg out of the Iselmeere, through the islands into the North Sea and along the north coast of Europe if the wind held in the north-west. We were only three hours sailing from the Kornworderzand locks and once through them we would not stop again until we reached Denmark if we could help it. We filled our tanks with water and petrol and looked in the almanac for the time of high water at the locks. If we passed through them at high water it would give us the whole of the ebb to get ourselves clear away into the North Sea. We estimated that if we left Stavoren at half past eleven we would be in the locks in plenty of time.

Shopping in the pretty town was a pleasure, with only a few yards to carry the baskets back on board. Celia's leg was much better. The swelling had gone down, the cuts had healed well and although her shin was one bulbous bruise she could walk without pain. Anne's bathing and bandaging every morning and evening was showing results. After several trips to the town with shopping baskets and cans Celia said "We're ready. There's enough to eat on board to last us for a fortnight". We went to the hotel again and found the barman just as pallid and sleepy in the clear light of day as he had been the previous evening. He gave us beer and two ice creams for the boys so that we could celebrate our departure from Holland. Then we took *Transcur* out of the harbour, waving good-bye to the old fishing boat, and headed north towards the locks. There was a moderate westerly wind and the sun shone brightly. Celia and I left Anne to steer and got out our new Dutch charts to plan the best route for us to take out into the North Sea. Outside the locks the Waddenzee looked a strange wild place. It is the strip of water between the great dyke across the Iselmeere and the Dutch Frisian Islands and it is a maze of shallows and sandbanks with only a few well defined deep water channels through it. The Dutch chart was coloured in pale blue with the drying sandbanks a deeper blue and the deep water channels in white. Texel over to the left and next to it Vlieland, then Terschelling, then Ameland form a crescent of long thin low sandy islands embracing in their span a strip of no-man's water twenty miles wide and sixty miles long between the islands and the north coast of Holland. The merest glance at the chart shows vast acres of drying sandbanks and one could see that it is as dangerous a piece of sea for a small sailing boat as it would be possible to find. It is more baffling even than the Thames Estuary which at least follows a logical pattern with all the sandbanks stretching like the fanning fingers of a great hand from the Thames outwards. In the Waddenzee the channels run across from east to west and outwards from the lock and from Harlingen eight miles to the eastward, between the islands and out to the North Sea. The channels are marked by a maze of buoys, beacons and withies which to a stranger make for confusion. Celia grinned. "I should hate to go aground out there on a falling tide" she said. We decided to go out through Zeetat van Terschelling between Vlieland and Terschelling Islands and then to turn to starboard and sail close to the north coast of Terschelling Island through the Noordgat and thence out into the North Sea. "For once we have got decent up-to-date charts" I said "There should be nothing difficult about it unless it comes in misty."

Two or three yachts were bound the same way as us and we followed them in the sunshine up towards the Kornworderzand. Soon we saw the dyke, picked out the entrance to the locks and tied up alongside the quay wall to wait for the gates to open. I looked at the big scale North Sea chart again and saw that when we did get out into the North Sea we would be a bare sixty miles nearer to Denmark than we had been when he had turned back to Ijmuiden. It was now Thursday morning so that it had taken us three days to cover that meagre distance.

"Don't worry about it" Celia said. "We still haven't been out a week and no one could say we haven't enjoyed seeing something of Holland. The trouble with you is you seem to see every cruise we make as a sort of challenge—to fulfil some programme you have fixed for yourself. Just take it easy. What does it matter if we're a few days late—or even if we don't get to Denmark at all? If we're all enjoying ourselves, surely that's enough?"

But I know she is wrong about this and it is something we shall never agree on. It isn't enough to wander aimlessly without any clear plan or purpose. I know that ashore I am at the mercy of circumstances I cannot control—pushed from compromise to compromise, from half-truth to half-lie, from one petty moral dishonesty to another by the ceaseless pressure to provide funds. But once away at sea all that is put aside. We have our plan and it is up to me whether we carry it out or not. For a few brief weeks I live honestly and am dealt with by the sea impartially, sometimes sternly, sometimes with exquisite gentleness but always with monumental justice. If I make mistakes the penalty is near at hand and if I am successful the reward, for all of us, is immediate. Ashore, the pressures of life work against me—the harsh fabric of society erodes the spirit. At sea I am free to treat with life in my own way, to take risks if they are justified but never to take liberties. It is half a battle with the sea and half with myself and the fight is as much one of wits and guile as of strength and endurance. One can be buffeted into a thousand pieces or the sea can defeat more subtly, by sowing indecision or lapses of confidence.

We were all ready to go out into the North Sea and we were all anxious to be making real progress towards Denmark once again. Our tanks were full of water and fuel, our food lockers were stuffed with provisions of every kind. The boys had enjoyed themselves in Holland with runs ashore, boats and windmills and new harbours to see and a new place to be explored every day. Under Anne's nursing Celia's leg had got better very quickly and she was able to walk without pain. Anne herself was full of pleasure at having been to an unexpected country and my own temper had been at least partially restored by the prospect of getting on again. We had all got well used to living on board—accustomed to the odd hours, the sleeping in snatches and to meals under way and at odd times. I felt, as I had felt two years

41

previously when the same five of us had been bound for Spain, that the boat was a sound and safe unit, able to withstand reverses and take full advantage of favourable circumstances. The children were happy and well and were enjoying themselves to the full. They were contented when confined to the boat and at the same time were full of interest and enthusiasm when let ashore. Successful cruising with two small children in the crew requires a good deal of adjustment and compromise on the part of the adults as well as the children, but we have often done it before and we know that the pleasure of having the children with us far outweighs the disadvantages. The life widens their experience and teaches us to value them as much for their restraint as for their exuberance. They will play quietly and happily for hours on end, devising their amusements ingeniously and when, occasionally, the moment comes for a romp they burst into life like dry kindling. They burn their energy and vitality at a prodigious rate during the day and stoke up with sleep at night ready for another release when morning comes. People go to endless lengths to dispose of their children while they enjoy themselves unencumbered when they go on holiday, but to us a holiday in the boat without the children would be empty of meaning. Sharing our experiences they know us for what we are.

Chapter Four

We had our lunch sitting peaceably round *Trans-cur*'s cabin table while we waited for the lock gates to open. The dyke stretched in a straight line for sixteen miles towards the south west and for two miles in the other direction to the eastern shore of the Iselmeere. The building of the dyke was a mammoth task—started in 1886 and not finished until 1932 when the sea was finally excluded and the Zuider Zee became the Iselmeere. At the end of the war the retreating German army did enormous damage to the sea defences in this part of Holland and although the Great Dyke was not destroyed they succeeded in inundating fifty thousand acres of precious farmland. When it was finally re-drained by the Dutch the countryside had been devastated and the land covered with a vast plain of mud. All this and much besides has helped the Germans to leave unpleasant memories in Holland which still persist, although memories soon fade into mythology. When Celia and I first came to Holland it was not so long after the end of the war and we were once briefly mistaken for Germans in a bar in Flushing; it was not a pleasant experience. Sensing the atmosphere we explained that we were English and then sullen hostility changed to friendliness.

Patrick finished his lunch first and went up on deck. "They're opening the gates", he called earnestly to us, "do hurry up. The boats are going in." We started the engine at once and passed into the lock together with two coasters and half a dozen yachts, one of them a magnificent white and varnished boyer. In a few minutes the water level was rising and soon the gates at the seaward end of the lock began to open. "Will the next place be Denmark?" Adrian asked, "Will we be there to-morrow?" The boys always think new places will be there for them the next day, regardless of how far off they may be; their feeling for time seldom spans more than a single day. Anne remarked ruefully, "Oh well, it wasn't a very long visit, but I did enjoy Holland" as she slammed the engine into gear and *Transcur* gathered way and passed out of the lock. There was a swing bridge immediately ahead of us, then a small patch of enclosed water, calm and nicely sheltered by the harbour mole, then the open Waddenzee, rough and uncompromising. As soon as we were past the swing bridge I began to hoist the mainsail. There was a strong wind from the west and I could see that we would have it right ahead of us until the first bend in the narrow winding channel, when another bend to starboard would allow us to fetch. The other yachts were making sail and I noticed that they all had reefs in their mainsails; all, that is, except the big boyer which was hoisting full sail. I knew that *Transcur* was a good bit stiffer than any of the other yachts and that she would carry her normal working sails without being overpressed. As soon as we were through the bridge Celia slowed the engine and I began to hoist the mainsail. The time was 1414.

The mainsail went up as far as the crosstrees and then it jammed solid and would not move up or down. I pulled hard on the halliard but the sail would not go up; I pulled down on the luff rope but it would not move. I looked aloft but the sun shone out of a clear sky, blinding me so that I could not distinguish one rope from another. The half hoisted sail was full of wind and was threshing and kicking violently "Put about" I shouted to Celia "Something's gone wrong." Celia turned *Transcur* tight round in the narrow space inside the mole and headed her back to the bridge, which by now was closed. There was

44

nothing to tie up to along the mole, it was impossible to drop the anchor in this narrow gut and outside the shelter of the mole we could see that the strong wind was kicking up a nasty sea. "I'll have to go aloft to clear it."

Celia kept the engine turning over slowly and strove to man-œuvre *Transcur* so that she remained stationary in the lee of the mole, while I climbed the ratlines. I could see nothing against the sun but I guessed that the wire halliard, above the downhaul block, had somehow become foul. I climbed up to the top of the shrouds and scrambled onto the crosstrees, disassociating myself from Celia's efforts and concentrating only on clearing the sail. I saw at once what had gone wrong. The mast-head halliard that we use for hoisting the big headsail had contrived to get its spring clip securely fastened to both parts of the main halliard so that it was jammed solid. By standing tiptoe on the crosstrees with an arm round the mast for support I was just able to reach the tangle. I spared a glance for *Transcur* and saw that she was going straight for the bridge again and that Celia was wildly turning in tight circles so that we would neither hit the bridge nor go out into the rough open sea where work aloft would be impos-sible. "Don't fall" she shouted more to satisfy her own fears, I reflected, than to contribute to my safety. I struggled with the snarled up rope and wire for five minutes while Celia kept *Transcur* precariously between the open sea and the bridge. When it was done I slid down the shrouds and Anne and I hoisted the main and broke out the jib as smartly as we knew how. *Transcur* shot from behind the protection of the mole and in seconds we were threshing to windward with the short seas breaking against the bow and sending spray stinging across the cockpit. We were in a narrow channel, copiously buoyed on each side, with the dyke stretching away to the horizon to port and to starboard a confusion of short, breaking, tidal, shallow seas. The other yachts were by now well ahead of us and we followed their lead and made short boards between the buoys. "This is a horrible place" Celia said when I had got my breath back "I only hope that little tangle was not prophetic." "Don't worry, we shall soon turn away to starboard and then we shall

45

have it free. Look, the first of them has already turned." The time was 1428.

We tacked along the narrow channel to the first corner, rapidly overhauling the other yachts. Anne was standing in the alleyway glued to the chart, checking off the numbered buoys as we came up with them, calling out the courses as we came to the corners and carefully noting the times in the log. The whole sea seemed to be a welter of buoys, so confusing that if we had not been following the other yachts we might well have lost our bearings. "Maybe it wasn't such bad luck getting the halliard jammed" I said to Celia "Otherwise we would have been first out, with no one to follow." The big boyer, her white paint and varnish glistening in the sun, with her lee-boards and her shallow draught, was making big boards right outside the channel and across the shallows, but the other yachts were keeping rigidly between the buoys with ourselves following close behind them. When we got into the Zuidoostrak we were able to relax a little and ten minutes later we eased the sheet and *Transcur* settled down to a fast pace which put two of the other yachts and the boyer behind us, leaving one larger and faster boat still in front. The time was 1522.

"Why did the halliard jam?" Celia asked. It had never happened before although when I came to think of it I wondered why it had not. "Because that spring clip on the headsail halliard is a bad piece of equipment which I should never have put there" I replied "It's a gadget." It is true that many of the fittings that are made for modern boats are more of a danger than an asset and that, generally speaking, in an old ship like *Transcur* you are better off with simple, orthodox fittings which may be more trouble to use but which cannot cause dangerous accidents. If we had been at sea in a lot of wind and if the sail had jammed when we were taking it down instead of hoisting it, we might have found ourselves in bad trouble. Usually, I try to keep our gear as simple and straightforward as I can but every now and then I see a splendid chromium plated fitting on the shelves of some yacht store and am carried away by it. There is no end to the clever gadgets that can be bought for a boat and sometimes in the winter when *Transcur* is laid up, a feeling of

46

nostalgia for the open sea comes over me and I dream up a new method of rigging some piece of gear and buy a gadget for doing it. But when it comes to the point, real boats are rigged with rope and wire and blocks and shackles and any extras are a needless fancy which you are better off without. "That'll teach you to go buying bits and pieces" Celia said reproachfully.

Now that we had the wind free we made good progress out towards the Zeegat van Terschelling, the passage between Terschelling and Vlieland, and soon we were able to see the low outline of the islands and the 170 foot high Terschelling lighthouse, the Brandaris Tower which is one of the oldest lighthouses in Northern Europe. The strong wind eased a little and we made very good progress although the last of the yachts which had been with us when we left the lock remained stubbornly ahead. "I think if we hoist the big headsail we could catch her", I said to Celia. She was against this plan and was dubious about hoisting the big sail. "We're going along quite nicely as we are," she said, "Why not just let well alone?" But the yacht ahead of us offered a challenge which I could not find it in myself to ignore. Half an hour passed and we were still quarter of a mile behind so I dragged Patrick away from a game he and Adrian were playing in the cabin and we set to work. We rolled up the working jib on its Wickham Martin roller, cleared away the halliard, hanked the sail to the forestay and hoisted it to the masthead. *Transcur* at once surged forward and Celia and Anne made tea while I watched happily as she began to gain foot by foot. The boys went back to their game—running cars out of the the the fo'c'sle and over the step into the saloon via a bridge they had made from pieces of plywood. As we finished our tea we were abreast of the yacht, a German cutter, and we all waved merrily to him and his companion as we sailed past. Then we came up to the junction of the Vliestroom and the West Meep and Anne and I concentrated on watching for the buoys. The sun went behind clouds and a thin mist came down, cutting visibility to no more than a quarter of a mile. The time was 1545.

Apart from the yachts in company with us we had seen nothing but a few Dutch fishing boats, some of them working far away from the channels, apparently in patches of deep water among the sand. "For sheer desolation this place takes a lot of beating," Anne remarked. The sea was a sandy brown colour and the edges of the shoals were marked by long lines of small curling breakers, steep and vicious by the looks of them. When the mist came down Celia put away the tea things and came up to help us. We had now turned off to starboard and were in a fierce cross current and the next buoy that we were looking for had failed to materialise. I set course on the compass 020 degrees, allowing as best I could for the current and Celia steered while Anne and I struggled to pierce the mist with our eyes. We had lost the other yachts now and were quite alone in a cold and friendless place.

As we got into the passage between the islands and cleared the lee of Vlieland the seas at once became steeper and the wind freshened. "I wish to God that sail was down" Celia muttered under her breath. I wished to God it was down as well. I wished I had never put it up—Celia is more than often right about these things yet some perversity in me prevents me from taking her advice—but I could do nothing about it now. "Wait till we get ourselves sorted out" I said "and I'll take it in." We seemed to run for an age without seeing a single buoy and the seas now were getting steeper as if the water was shallow. Every now and then one would curl up over the weather rail and tumble across the deck and you could hear quite clearly through the mist a low rumbling noise—something like an endless railway train—in the distance. The railway train noise, we knew, was made by breakers on a drying sand. "I don't like this at all" Celia said, "I think we ought to turn back and go out through the other channel." Certainly there was another channel, a much easier one, which would also take us out into the North Sea—the Zeegat van Ter- schelling—but it was a longer way round by a good fifteen miles and now that we had been running free for half an hour it was to windward of us.

The channel I was proposing to use was the Boomkensdiep which curved round close to the northern shore of Terschelling Island. After about four miles this channel splits into two parts, the Thomas Smit gat turning away to the north and the Noordgat still keeping close to the island for another three or four miles. The chart showed a minimum depth of fifteen feet in the Noordgat at low water springs and it was this channel that I had decided to take. Although the Thomas Smit gat was wider and appeared from the chart to be easier, it had written across it on the chart the words "Closed to navigation". As the chart had only been bought four days previously in the main Dutch Chart-Depot in Amsterdam and as I had been assured by the officer there that it was corrected up to date, I saw no reason to doubt its accuracy. Very often, the charts we use are years out of date and uncorrected and so I had implicit faith in this bright new Dutch one. The Amsterdam Chart Depot had appeared to be such a highly efficient place that I thought the chart could be trusted without question. I was on the point of agreeing with Celia and altering the course, hauling in the sheets and starting the beat back to the other passage, when Anne heard the whistle of a buoy through the mist. The time was 1635

I dived into the cabin to check against the chart, although I knew quite well which buoy it was. It was marked clearly "Stortmelk, Whistle" and it sounded as if it was on our port bow. We had evidently been carried slightly faster than we had reckoned by the strong ebb tide and the freshening wind but a small alteration would put us right in the mouth of the Boomkensdiep. "There it is" Patrick cried out and just as the next mournful whistle floated across the sea to us we all saw it looming out of the mist not more than two hundred yards away, gently heaving its barnacled sides up and down on the seas and gyrating on its mooring as the strong current swept past it, tearing at it and worrying it and doing all it could to wrench it from the sea bed and carry it in triumph out to open water. There was no mistaking it—black and white vertical stripes and a top mark—and so we bore away another 10 degrees, bringing the wind almost aft and concentrating our attentions on finding the next buoy.

"We shall be all right now," I said to Celia, "this channel is buoyed and we just keep close to the land right round until we're clear." Indeed, the mist had lifted a little and we could just see the outline of the shore on our starboard side. "That's a relief, I didn't like that for a minute or two" I admitted. Ten minutes later we picked up the next channel buoy. Adrian came out of the companionway. "Can we have a story Mummy?" he asked "You promised you would read to us after tea." Anne agreed to read to them as soon as she had finished the washing up which Celia had left half done on the engine box. Suddenly everything was quiet and peaceful again and the tensions of the last quarter of an hour evaporated. The channel was clearly marked and *Transcur* was sailing fast with the wind aft. The seas were quite big and they came bubbling and foaming up alongside the cockpit as we rushed to the eastward. "I'll set the log as soon as we get clear" I said. "What about taking in the big sail?" "Oh well, we might as well leave it where it is for the time being. It's pushing her along at a great speed." We must have been doing all of six knots with a brisk fair breeze and the tide under us. The shore could still be seen dimly through uncertain light and the remains of mist and the channel buoys bobbed up regularly. We could hear Anne reading aloud to the boys in the cabin. There was a steady swishing noise as *Transcur* threw the water away from her bows; a flock of small birds came sweeping past us in tight formation, skimming across the waves and weaving from side to side in response to some mute command. *Transcur* would surge forward on the crest of a wave, pause for an instant, dip her bowsprit and surge forward again. She was steering easily with the wind just on the port quarter and the sails were pulling well but not straining, with the big headsail alternately billowing out and then falling slack as the mainsail took the wind from it. The time was 1710. After another quarter of an hour we came to another buoy, bigger than those we had been passing, with a top mark on it, and beyond, we could see no more buoys.

"This'll be where the two channels meet" I said "I'll just go down and check the course." I slid the parallel rules across the chart yet again and read off the course, 055 degrees. There could be no mistake about it. Our position was clear, the Thomas Smit Gat was closed to navigation and therefore the Noordgat was the only possible passage. I set the new course and we altered

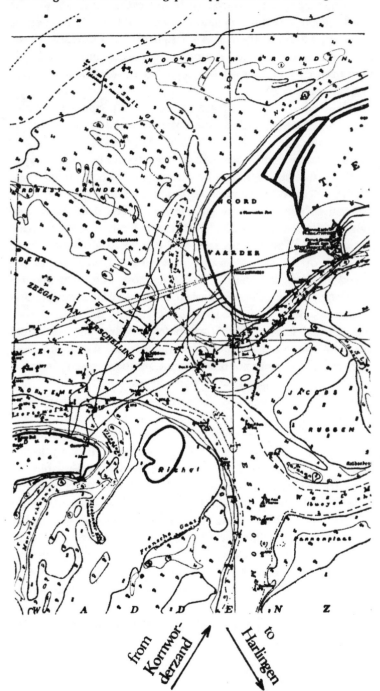

a few more degrees to starboard bringing the wind almost dead aft. Visibility was still very bad but we could see the land out to starboard although there was no sign of the Brandaris Tower which was now on the other side of the island from us. It would have been easy to see over the low coast in reasonable visibility. The time was 1730.

Celia and I stood in silence in the cockpit. She was steering and I was leaning against the companion hatch straining my eyes into the misty evening. The seas were not big but they were growing steeper, the tops falling over themselves like a girl's tightly curled hair. We began to hear the railway train again out to port. "Bear away as much as you can without gybing" I said "We must be a bit too far off the shore. The deep water runs right close up to the beach." "All right. I can give her another five degrees". The seas became even steeper as we went on and the noise of the railway train grew louder. I went down and looked again at the chart. The Terschelling bank was about a mile long, shaped like a squashed kidney with its longest and shallowest side towards the shore. At one point the chart showed that it dried five feet but immediately towards the land from this point the water was deep and the channel was a good half a mile wide. We were not more than a quarter of a mile from the shore so that there just must be water for us.

"Frank, I don't like this" I heard Celia say, quietly but with a certain pitch in her voice that told me she was really alarmed. I had heard her speak in that way two or maybe three times before since we have been sailing together. "I don't like it either. I'll take a sounding." I jumped up on to the cabin top where the lead lies coiled neatly on the deck forward of the companion hatch and I had my hand on it when *Transcur* struck the Terschelling bank, bringing up all standing with a thud like a pile-driver and a shudder which shook her right through from stem to stern. I heard Celia say "Oh my God" and then she ran down into the cabin to the children. Patrick came past her in the alleyway, up to the companionway so that I could see his anguished face looking up at me. "Daddy," he cried "Daddy what's happened?" Then the first big sea struck her blunt square stern. The weight of it swept on board, rolled over the after-deck, tumbled across the coaming, down into the cockpit and through the companionway. The spray from it leapt high in the air and came stinging across the cockpit and straight through the companionway. Spray and sea hit Patrick together, bowling him off his feet and throwing him back into the cabin. The time was 1805.

Chapter Five

The next sea was heavier and green water came surging over the stern, rumbled into the cockpit and through into the cabin. I saw this wave out of the corner of my eye, the vicious curving crest, coloured a light brown by tiny suspended particles of sand, seemed to hover for an instant high up above *Transcur*'s stern and then, quite deliberately, it moved in like a great foaming hound converging for the kill. The top half of it crashed down on the afterdeck, and at the same time the bottom half lifted the stern, swinging it to port. The tiller was wrenched over and its carved head was forced right across the boat and down into the scuppers. *Transcur* gybed, the heavy boom and the sail crashing with tremendous force across the boat. As the sail brought up against the sheet, whipping the parts of the rope like pieces of string, the stern lifted once more, she slewed round again and as she came down her stern post crashed into the sand so that it seemed that it must be driven right up through the counter. I heard Patrick's startled cry from the cabin and Celia's calm voice, "It's all right boys, don't worry it'll be all right soon."

Then *Transcur* lay over on her port side, turned away from the seas now so that the breaking crests cascaded over her. With each new wave she lifted again and then pounded down onto

54

the sand, the tiller kicking wildly and smashing itself into the lee scuppers. My first impulse was to drop the anchor to prevent *Transcur* from driving further onto the sand but first I knew I had to secure the tiller before the rudder was wrenched off its hangings. I fought with it as if it were a ferocious animal and strove to get it amidships so that I could fasten the tiller lines round it, but with the strength of a tiger it wrenched itself from side to side in fury. Celia came out, "Hang on to it as hard as you can while I get a line round it." There was a length of heavy shock cord in the cockpit locker and I lashed the tiller with this so that the elastic cord would take some of the strain. "Now I'm going to get the anchor down. Get the children into life jackets and you and Anne put them on as well." The deck was swept with water as I went forward and climbed over the dinghy into the bows. I could feel the boat lifting and pounding down onto the sand. The mast was shaking, the massive bowsprit was whipping like a willow twig, the deck seemed to have taken on a new personality of its own and was intent on throwing me off my feet. As luck would have it the anchor fairlead was on the lee side and I knew I could not drop the anchor there, as *Transcur* would tend to move to leeward and soon she would be sitting on top of it. I hauled chain out of the locker, leaving it loose on the deck, and dropped the anchor over the stem. Then I climbed out on to the bobstay, grabbed the chain underneath the stay and hauled the anchor up on to the deck on the weather side. I struggled aft with the anchor and slack chain in my hands and from the shrouds I threw it out as far as I could to windward. It took me ten minutes to get the anchor away and it gave me ten minutes in which to think. When I climbed back into the cockpit I was soaked through and bleeding from a small cut on my hand, but I had a plan. "How are those poor bloody boys getting on?" I asked Celia. "Not too bad. They're frightened, but Anne is reading to them. Are you going to let off flares? We must get them out of this."

I reached into the cabin and switched on the electric pump, heard it suck water and looked over the weather side to see that the bilge water was running out through the discharge. Now that

55

she was lying over the surf beat against the weather side of the hull and most of the water that came over the rail flooded right across the deck and down into the sea to leeward. She was pounding continuously and it seemed impossible that she could stand this treatment for long. Already she was leaking badly—the bilge water was lying three or four inches deep over the port side of the cabin floor.

"Celia, you and Anne must go ashore with the children in the life raft. The wind will blow you towards the beach. You'll be there in half an hour. When you get ashore you'll have to try and get a lift or hire a taxi and go into Terschelling to get someone out here to tow us off. I'll stay here and keep the boat pumped out. You never know, I might get her off. If things get too bad I'll put up flares. I'm not going to leave her now but you must go and find help and get the children ashore. This is no place for the boys. They're used to everything being just right in this boat and they'll never understand this."

Celia was full of uncertainty and hesitancy about this plan. "We can't go off and leave you here alone" she said, but the logic of the situation was inescapable. The children were frightened and they had to be put ashore without delay. Equally, I refused to put up distress signals until it was quite clear that *Transcur* was going to founder, "It's astonishing that she's still in one piece now" I said "You never know, she might come off." I had no wish to leave the boat if there was a chance of saving her or to face a salvage claim unless there was no other way out. If the worse came to the worst, if no help came and I was unable to get her afloat, I knew I would be able to get ashore with a life belt round me. "Get everyone ready to go" I said "and in five minutes I'll launch the Tern."

I went forward again, let go the halliard for the big headsail, brought in the forestay and hauled the sail down stuffing it in a wet heap on the lee side of the fore deck. *Transcur* had now swung broadside to the surf and she seemed to be lying a little more easily. She was pointing towards deeper water and I thought that if I left the mainsail up it might tend to move her forward. The wind seemed to have eased a little and I could see the vague

56

outline of the sandy shore over the bow. In every other direction there was a waste of breaking water, a desolation of boiling surf unrelieved by any living thing. I worked my way aft and went to the yellow life raft lying in its container across the after deck abaft the cockpit coaming. The wooden pin which secured the raft had seized solid between the wet and shrunken lashings that held it in place and I had to get out my knife and cut it adrift. I made quite sure that the raft's tripping line was securely fast and then I lifted it up and hurled it into the sea to leeward, giving the line a sharp jerk as I did so. For a moment it lay in the sea half submerged in its container. "Damn it," I said "this bloody thing isn't going to work." Then, in a moment, there was a hissing noise and it began to unfold like a great yellow flower. I watched it take shape gradually, first the round perimeter blew up like a German sausage and then the hood and canopy took shape so that in a few seconds I was holding the painter of a fully fledged boat. By the looks of it, it was a seaworthy craft.

Celia was in the cabin explaining to Anne and the boys what we had decided. The boys were sitting on the lee bunk their feet awash with bilge water and Anne was between them reading a chapter of their book. Adrian was silent and pale but Patrick, soaking wet, was full of questions as soon as Celia came below. "Will it be all right, Mummy?" "Why is all this water on the floor?" "Is Daddy managing all right?" He was little worse for his wetting and Anne had managed to put some dry clothes on him. "We're all going ashore in the life raft" Celia told them, "We must take a bag with us and you can take your bears. Then when Daddy gets Transcur off the sand we'll all meet in Terschelling." Adrian accepted this without comment but Patrick asked at once "Why are we going ashore if Daddy's going to get Transcur off?" "So that we can send someone out from Terschelling to help him." They busied themselves collecting their most valued possessions and Celia packed their things into a small zipper bag. She put in some chocolate, her cigarettes and a bottle of brandy from the drink locker. Anne came out to the companionway to get a cup from one of the galley lockers just as I was throwing the life raft overboard. "Are you going to be all right yourself?" she asked, "Shouldn't I stay with you?" "No, you'll have to go and help Celia with the boys." She was anxious yet calm but I noticed that her hands shook as she reached into the locker. The boys put their oilskins on over their life jackets. They were buttoned up and the belts fastened so that they looked like small spacemen. Adrian's worried eyes looked anxiously out from under the brim of his sou'wester. They glanced round with apprehension at the familiar articles of their life that they were leaving behind—books, toys, model boats, everything that went towards making *Transcur* their home.

As soon as the life raft had inflated itself the wind took it and it began to surge away in the surf. A sea hit it and flooded through the opening in the canopy, filling it with water so that it became very heavy to hold although it still appeared to be buoyant. The next time a sea took it the thin nylon tripping line, which was now the painter, was wrenched through my hands with tremendous force. Fortunately, I had previously fastened a thicker length of terylene rope to the painter, as I had doubted whether it would otherwise have been long enough, and I was able to hold this with a turn round one of the stanchions for the boom crutch. At the same time, the strain on it was terrific every time the raft was taken away by a sea, and every minute I expected the painter to be torn away from its fastening on the raft. I knew it wouldn't break but I doubted the strength of its attachment to the raft. It was clearly out of the question for anyone to board the raft in this position, let alone small children.

I shouted to Celia in the cabin "You'll have to get on to the raft from the foredeck. When I shout, come forward with Patrick. Anne can follow with Adrian when you are safely on board." The raft was now streaming out to leeward on about twenty feet of painter and I was easing it away when the seas caught it and pulling it in again when a lull came. I worked my way forward up the lee scuppers under the boom, playing the raft like a fisherman with a twenty pound salmon, until I was able to crouch down just forward of the shrouds and take a turn with the painter round one of the cleats inside the bulwarks. Then I hauled the raft alongside taking in the slack on the painter as the strain came off it and paying out as a sea hit the raft. It looked an uninviting craft to put to sea in, I thought as I shouted for Celia to come forward. She came up the weather side to the fore deck with her little bag and Patrick holding tightly to her hand "You squat down here beside me" I said to Patrick "while Mummy gets in." I managed to manœuvre the raft round so that the opening in the canopy was towards *Transcur* "Off you go" I said, "Watch it." Celia swung her legs over the rail and the next time the raft came up on a wave she jumped and disappeared under the canopy. Then a much bigger sea took the raft and swept it away forward so that I had to pay out on the painter until it was almost out to the bare end, and the raft, with Celia in it, was heaving up and down on the waves right out clear of the bowsprit.

Now that Celia was aboard the raft, the strain on the painter was much greater and every time a wave caught it the thin nylon cord stretched bar tight like a guitar string and I could see it tugging at the rubber fastening where it was attached to the raft. I had a horrible vision of Celia being carried away by herself, separated from the children who would be left on board with no means of saving themselves if *Transcur* should founder. The painter cut into my hands as I worked the raft back alongside, hauling in when a lull came and paying out again when a wave would suddenly jerk it and put an impossible strain on it.

Patrick was perfectly calm. "It's a jolly good raft" he said, "Look how well it rides over the waves." I could see Celia trying to bale the raft out with her hands as I pulled her alongside. "There should be a bailer in it" I shouted to her. "I know, but it's tied up in a bag and I can't get the lashing undone." After what seemed an age the raft was alongside again. "Are you ready, I'll pass him over to you." I caught a turn with the painter and when the raft rose alongside on a sea I grabbed Patrick and heaved him over the rail, feet first, into Celia's outstretched hands. She seized hold of him and hauled him down into the raft. "Mummy, it's full of water but there's a fine place to sit" I heard him say. I shouted out to Anne and a moment later she

59

was beside me with Adrian. "You go first and then I'll pass Adrian down." Anne watched for her chance, slid neatly over the rail and disappeared under the canopy. By now the raft was very heavy and was jerking and kicking at the painter so that I thought something must break. It came up on a sea and I saw my chance, caught hold of Adrian and pushed him over the rail. Celia, half standing half kneeling on the edge of the raft stretched out her arms for him and just at that moment a vicious surf came bubbling up alongside and the raft began to sheer away. Adrian was halfway over, his feet held firmly by Celia and my hands under his shoulders. The sea came foaming up all round us with a muffled hissing noise and for a moment we were all smothered in boiling spray. The raft began to swing away from *Transcur* and I had to let Adrian go. I had a glimpse of Celia's face as she heaved him in, soaking wet, pale but quiet. "You all right love?" I heard her say to him. "Yes Mummy" he murmured "I'm all right." I slipped the painter and let it run out through my hands, first the thin nylon line, then the terylene rope and finally I held the bare end for an instant before the next wave jerked it away and they were gone. "Good-bye, good luck." I caught a glimpse of Celia's face before they were gone and it had on it a look of unmitigated sadness which overlaid the expression of concern. You have to know how to love before you can feel real sadness like that. They are part of the same thing.

The sea and the wind took the raft quickly away and I watched as it floated off into the thick of the worst surf, gyrating slowly round so that sometimes I could only see the yellow canopy and sometimes it would swing round towards me so that I could see Celia and Anne sitting in the opening and doing something with their hands—either bailing or attempting to paddle towards the shore, I could not make out which. They seemed to be going down the coast and parallel to it instead of towards the shore and a feeling of utter hopelessness came over me as I saw them carried into the very worst part of the surf where the shallow, sandy water was being kicked up in a fury by the racing tide and the wind. They seemed to be headed straight for a patch of water that was incredibly rough and dangerous—pinnacles of water leaping into the air like performers in some devil's dance, spray and spume flying in all directions and the grumbling noise, louder now than ever, endlessly moaning. "Oh my Christ, now I've done it—they're going out to sea." Now I saw what a crass bloody idiot I had been, I'd sent them out to sea instead of to the shore. Surely to Christ the wind must blow them towards the beach? But the tide was now far stronger than the wind and for every yard they made towards the shore they were carried ten along the coast. "If they pass that point without getting ashore they're done—they'll be in the North Sea, miles from any shipping and with the dark coming down."

I sat in the cockpit and watched them as *Transcur* lifted and banged down on the sand and I suddenly felt tired and wet and cold and utterly dispirited. Now I had committed the supreme error of judgment—the ultimate blunder. Here I was, sitting on board *Transcur*, stunned by the enormity of my misjudgment, while everything in the world I held of any value was twisting and turning its way towards immediate destruction or, at best, towards a slow agony of exposure. There was no hope and no fight left in me as I sat in *Transcur*'s cockpit surrounded by the familiar timbers that were fast being torn apart under me so that soon I would be left with nothing but the life belt lying neatly round the top of the rudder post. I was suffering a crisis of confidence in my own ability to deal with life as I watched the results of my own errors developing into what might well become a major disaster. Huddled in the lee of the cockpit I reached into the cabin listlessly and took out the binoculars. Through the lenses I could see the raft growing rapidly more distant and occasionally Celia's form would swing into focus leaning over the side of it and paddling with her hands, trying to grasp the slippery surface of the sea to pull herself towards the beach.

I was not frightened, because I have never been frightened of the sea. I accept it as a friend or as an enemy and expect from it only what it is prepared to give, without regret or rancour. But I was filled with an overpowering sense of hopelessness. My mind flashed back to the last time I was face to face with the prospect

61

of drowning and I remembered that then, as now, I had felt this hollowness inside and the same sense of inevitability. It had been during the war, and I remembered that the hollowness had come within the space of a few seconds between the instant I had seen the phosphorescent wake of a torpedo speeding towards the ship and the dull impact of the explosion which had sounded just like the shudders that wracked *Transcur* now. I had been stupified into inactivity in just the same way then as now, standing nonplussed as I watched the ship stagger and then slowly begin to topple. Then, I had seen the captain, whom I respected with all the idealism of youth, walking across the lower bridge, carefully adjusting the angle of his gold braided cap and buttoning his immaculate white tunic, and this had released something inside me and had allowed me to take action—to regain incisiveness. Then, I had carried out mechanically the drill that had been dinned into me—to the chart room, get the heavy box of secret codes and papers, struggle to the wing of the bridge with it and hurl the perforated iron box over the side—a useless waste of time in the circumstances but what I had been taught was my part in this disaster. Then I had gone back to the chart room and collected a sextant in its mahogany box, a copy of the nautical almanac and a chart of the South Atlantic Ocean showing our position 500 miles from the African coast, and a copy of Burton's navigation tables. By the time I got out on to the bridge again the old ship was listing over and preparing herself for the last plunge. The boat deck was empty except for a round full moon hanging, it seemed, just over the funnel, and I could see the life boat swinging crazily on its falls far below. The men were already clearing away the hooks and preparing to get away. A rope ladder hung down from the edge of the deck, suspended in space like a big top trapeze and I swung myself over the side and started the dizzy descent, hampered by a cumbersome selection of books, the chart, and the sextant. The bottom of the ladder was still resting in the boat, the falls were free and the boat was only held to the ship by a lazy painter leading up to the fore deck. I heard the Captain shout "Hang on to that painter until the boy's down. I'll murder the man who lets that painter go." I had struggled on down, the boat swinging away from the ship until only the last rung of the ladder was still inboard, held grimly by a Maltese fireman. Then my feet were in the boat, I dropped the sextant and the books on board and was left clinging to the ladder with my legs held firmly from below, just as Adrian had been suspended between *Transcur* and the life raft. "Let go, you silly little bugger." A moment later I was in the boat, the painter was free and the ship, still carrying her way, was rushing past us. The poop was already awash and I saw in the moonlight that the gunner had leapt into the sea, only to be swept up by the back-wash and carried back on board to his death.

All that is years away in the past and I had hardly thought of it until this moment when it all came vividly back. The values of those days are gone side by side with the experiences and now one remembers the experiences but not the set of values that made them possible. The world then seemed all in black and white, good and bad, so that every choice was clear and easy to grasp. Not so now. The issues have become confused so that half of me is on one side and half on the other. What was right then is no longer right. We can no longer fight barbarism because we have made ourselves into barbarians worse than any that have gone before us. The only fight that has meaning is that of the poor against the privileged, the weak against the strong.

I had lost sight of the raft, it was gone into the misty confused turmoil where the sea and the sky merged together in an ill-defined emulsion. I began to think about leaving *Transcur*, my eyes went to the life belt sitting so snug round the rudder post and I wondered how the sea would feel and how I could manage to get through the surf into calmer water and then to the shore. I knew it would be useless to launch the dinghy in such a sea. I looked into the cabin and saw that the water was now right over the floor and was fast creeping up to the level of the tops of the bunks. Everything was in derelict confusion and, so quickly, all the neat discipline had gone from our boat. It struck me that the game was up and that the boat was finished—in fact it didn't seem worth the trouble of making any effort to save her. I took the glasses for a last look round and could see no sign of life

63

in the sea—nothing but a lone gull sweeping to and fro effortlessly above the breaking water. Then I swung the glasses towards the shore and suddenly four figures sprang into the lenses, walking through the shallows to the beach pulling the life raft behind them. First Anne, then Adrian, then Celia and then Patrick. "Christ, it's not true. It's not possible—they're ashore."

Chapter Six

"While you've been sitting here in a dream, you crazy idiot," I shouted to myself "those girls have got the children ashore. Christ, in an hour's time there'll be someone out here to tow the old boat off." I jumped into the cabin. The electric pump was still running but the water was gaining fast on the cabin floor, slip-slopping from side to side as *Transcur* heaved herself back and forth. I looked over the side and saw that the pump discharge was dry. "My God, the pump's blocked up—and you, you bloody idiot, you've been sitting here letting it burn itself out." I switched off the pump to save the little nylon impeller which would soon run hot and melt if no water was running through the pump to keep it lubricated. There was too much bilge water on the cabin floor to allow me to reach the screws securing the floor boards, so that I could take them out, lift the floor board and get at the pump intake in the bilge.

Now I was in a desperate hurry and every minute counted. I took the handle of the Vortex pump from its place, threaded it through the hole in the floor boards and felt for the key-way in the top of the pump. I found it by luck, and felt the handle engage. Then I sat down in the water, my legs stretched out before me with the pump handle sticking up between them and started to turn. I turned the handle and heard the water gushing out of the discharge pipe on the deck. "Now, you bastard, you just turn that pump handle and go on turning it until the goddamm water's gone." I turned for five minutes and then I began to tire. I slackened the pace, turning more slowly but getting rhythm into it, backwards and forwards, backwards and forwards. The words of the advertising leaflet came back to me "Moves one ton of water in seven minutes." "Yes, maybe it does if anybody is strong enough to turn it for seven minutes." I turned on and on, the sweat pouring out of me mingling with the bilge water, salt with salt. I turned until the whole world was turning with me, round and round it wheeled, rhythmically and smoothly, like the ceiling of a room after love-making. Sometimes it was the rest of the world that was going round and sometimes it was I and everything else was still. I felt my heart pounding inside my ribs, a bird battering at the bars, and I turned the pump until everything went blue and gold, rushing past my eyes. "Have a rest, you silly sod, you'll kill yourself."

I stopped turning and lay for a moment leaning against the door of Adrian's cabin. Then I saw that the water level had gone down to well below the level of the bunks. I raised myself up out of the water and groped in the cockpit locker for a screwdriver, then I took out the four stainless steel screws that hold the floor board in place. The board floated away into the cabin and I put my hand down into the bilge water and groped for the suction pipe of the electric pump. I found it and ran my hand along it until I came to the end where a small length of perforated copper pipe was joined to the plastic hose. Sure enough, the holes in the copper pipe were all jammed up with tiny particles of wood and dirt that had been shaken down into the bottom of the bilge. I cleared it, turned on the switch and went out on deck to look over the side. Fine, the pump still works, she's pumping out, a steady stream of water is flowing overboard.

I breathed deeply and wiped the oil and muck from my face. "Now, the sail's got to come down. If she's going to come off she must be heeling over the other way and she won't as long as the sail's full of wind." If she were heeled over to starboard instead of to port her propeller would be fully submerged and

66

there would be some hope of moving her with the engine. I went forward to the mast, let go the halliard and pulled the sail down. Then I got tyers from the cockpit locker, bound up the sail and lashed the boom into the crutch. With the sail down *Transcur* lifted herself until she was nearly upright but now she was not lying so easily and every time a wave swept under her she raised herself maybe a foot off the sand and then came crashing down again with a horrifying thud. "You poor old lady, you can't stand much of this."

I remembered that I had thrown the anchor overboard and I looked to see if I could follow the chain to where it was lying. The chain now seemed to be leading right underneath the boat and when I looked out to windward I could just see where the anchor was, lying in the sand not more than about eight feet out on the weather side. I had put the anchor out, thinking it would stop *Transcur* from driving higher onto the sand—it was an instinctive reaction to me to put the anchor out when you run ashore—but now she had swung round so that all it would do was to prevent her from coming off and I knew that I had to get it back inboard again even if it meant going overboard to fetch it, which, all else failing, I could have done. I thought of slipping the cable over the side and leaving the anchor where it was but I couldn't quite bring myself to do this without at least a good try to get it back. I reached for the chain with the boat-hook, hooked round it, and followed the chain along until I could almost touch the anchor. Then, by leaning over the side with my feet jammed under the cockpit coaming to keep me from falling head first into the sea, I probed with the boat hook at full stretch. By luck the hook caught under the bar across the fluke of the anchor. I pulled with all my might and then I pulled again, harder, but in my attenuated position I couldn't put much weight behind the pull and only the puny force of my arms was working for me. "Now come on you weak bloody article, one more pull." I heaved again with all my force and suddenly it was coming—everything was coming—there was a lurch—the anchor was much closer and the boat-hook came loose in my hands. "Christ, you've pulled the bloody boat over." By some incredible fortune, *Trans-*

cur had been caught by a rogue wave from the lee side and with the force of my pull against the anchor she had come upright, hovered for an instant and then fallen over to windward, just the way I wanted her to be. Now the anchor was five feet nearer to me and I dragged and fought at it until it suddenly came free of the sand. I levered the boat-hook down over the taffrail and pulled at the same time and suddenly it was there, above the water, and I grabbed at it, letting the boat-hook slip through my fingers and slither into the sea. But I had the anchor back on board.

I flopped down exhausted on the side decks and rested my head in my hands over the rail with my eyes closed. The waves were now slopping up on board and washing right over me but I was exhausted and it was only the cold sea water slapping hard into my face that caused energy to flood back into me. I did not resent the water, I was already wet and it is not possible to be more wet than wet, rather I welcomed each new wave as a friend. I opened my eyes and as the light sent its message painstakingly back into my brain I found myself looking down into the sea like a sick drunk retching over the side of the Calais packet. The discharge from the electric pump was just under me and it came into my consciousness that only a thin dribble of water was coming lazily out. Perhaps she had pumped herself dry and everything would be all right again. Maybe I ought to go inside and have a look, but it was so nice and restful lying here with the spray flying over me and occasionally a refreshing green wave. Of course, the little nylon impeller of the pump must be whirring round inside its chamber. If no water is coming through, it will begin to get hot and soon the nylon will reach its melting point and then it will go soft, and after a few more minutes of whizzing round it will disintegrate and then the shaft will race round, having shaken the impeller free, and the motor will get hot and the commutator will start to burn and everything will be warm and dry and comfortable, like sitting in front of a great log fire at home, and maybe Patrick would play the piano, his sensitive fingers finding their way surprisingly accurately for a little boy, among the white and black notes. Perhaps Celia would bring a cup of tea, or perhaps a drink. "A drink. Christ, that's what you want, a drink. There's a bottle of brandy in the locker. Go and get it you great lazy bastard—go and get your own bloody drink."

I pulled myself up out of the scuppers and went below. *Transcur* was still half full of water and the pump was still whirring. I switched it off, went into the saloon, reached behind my bunk for the brandy—but the bottle had gone. "Now who in Christ's name has taken that bottle? Oh God, of course, Celia's got it. Celia's ashore. I saw her walking up the beach. She'll be sending someone out to tow me off this bloody Terschelling bank." There was a whisky bottle there and I poured myself half a tumbler full and drank it down. The spirit scorched my throat and carried on down into my stomach, making me shiver as it spread through me like penetrating oil, finally working its way into my brain and opening up the numbed tissues. I went up on deck, made my way forward to the topping lift and pulled on it so that the boom lifted from the crutch and swung over onto the side *Transcur* was now leaning—that would help to keep her heeling over the way I wanted her. Then I went back to the cabin, found the pump lead again and cleaned the little pieces of wood out from the hose in the copper rose. When I switched on I heard it pick up its suction and I knew the water was running out again. Then I sat down on the floor again and began to turn the Vortex pump but this time I did it in short bursts—twenty turns only, then rest, then twenty turns again, then rest. This was a more sensible way to pump a boat out, and I went on until I began to get a stitch in my side so that it became too painful to turn the pump handle. But the water had gone down appreciably so that it was not more than four inches over the cabin floor. "Now, if we hadn't dropped the floor this season, that water would be underneath it in the bilge. We're winning."

I went up into the cockpit and looked round to see if there was any sign of the boat Celia would be sending out from Terschelling, but nothing was to be seen but empty sea and mist and a low line ahead of me where the shore was. It was nearly dark by now and a few stars shone dimly overhead. The wind had shifted more northerly and was blowing stronger, possibly force five, and kicking up such a sea on the sand bank that I marvelled that *Transcur* could stand the pounding. I had got used to the noise by now and it did not terrify me as it had done when we first struck the sand. She would pick her stern post up and grind it into the sand. Sometimes when she fell back she seemed to muzzle into it quite comfortably, with no more than a shudder as she ground her keel into it, but sometimes she would lift more and she would drop down on the sand like a bag of cement falling on to a stone floor. Then the boat would shake with the tremendous impact of her whole weight—about seven tons—dropping dead onto the bottom. Every time that happened the tiller kicked against its shock cord lashings and gave a spiteful lunge in one direction or the other. "This poor bloody rudder can't last much longer." All around was broken water except for a patch ahead of me that seemed to be calmer. I wondered whether she had moved since I got in the anchor.

Then I thought of the tide. "Of course, it must be flooding by now. Maybe she'll move." I went inside and turned on the petrol, then I flooded the carburettor and pressed the self starter. The engine roared into life at once, as it always did and I increased the revs and threw the gear lever ahead. The engine spluttered and roared as she rose on the surf and the propeller broke the surface, then when she dropped the propeller bit into the water. I looked over the side. "Jesus Christ she's moving. She's going ahead." She was moving inch by inch as she rose on the surf. I could swear she was moving. The engine was vibrating and shaking on its mountings when the propeller raced so that I had to go inside and stand by it, easing the throttle as it roared and shook and opening it out whenever the propeller bit deep into the water. Suddenly as I stood by the engine, the pounding ceased and *Transcur* was upright. "She's afloat, she's afloat, she's afloat" I shouted as loud as I could. I eased the throttle again, threw the lever into neutral, flew to the tiller lashings and pulled the two loops of shock cord away. Then I looked about me in the failing light.

I was in a sort of lagoon in the sand bank. As far as I could see the surf and broken water was all round me and there did not seem to be any way through into deep water. Behind me was the main part of the Terschelling bank with the waves leaping and cavorting dementedly and in front of me there was another line of surf. As far as I could see in the failing light the lagoon was about twenty yards wide and fifty yards long but across the surf towards the shore the water was calmer and I knew it was deep in that direction, between me and the shore, if only I could get over the surf bank. The wind was blowing *Transcur* fast towards the line of broken water. I put the helm hard down to swing her round clear of it but as she started to turn she struck again. Her bow at once paid off with the wind and she lifted once again and crashed down onto the sand. "Not again" I muttered "Don't for God's sake do this to me again." But she was hard on the sand again doing her best to pound herself to pieces just as she had done before. "You're playing with me you old bitch"I swore at her as I had never done before and I felt tears of frustration and disappointment rolling down my cheeks. I felt the old sense of hopelessness returning and I had to fight it back. "Don't give up now, don't give up now." I put the engine into reverse but it only shook and roared and threshed uselessly. She was hard on again and heeling over to starboard as before but this time she lifted and fell back onto the sand even more fiercely than before. I thought that I would fail—that nothing would get her off again and that at last she would break up and be lost.

I left the tiller to kick itself to pieces and went back in the cabin, stepping through the alleyway across the bearers for the floor boards and into the saloon where the water was already climbing up again towards the bunks. "This is the finish of it. We've had a good old try but if you won't bloody well come you might as well stay here and rot your bones." I knew just how she would go. First, one of the planks in the bottom, at the turn of the bilge, which was taking all the punishment, would spring away from the timbers—or maybe she would come down one of these times on a stone or a small piece of rock which would punch a hole right through her. Then there would be no question

71

of pumping—the water would flood in and she would settle firmly and comfortably in the sand and finally be still. Then the sea would begin its inexorable task of demolition, gradually breaking pieces of her planking away and carrying off the loose gear from inside, small piece by small piece. The first gale that came would make a clean sweep of anything moveable. I could imagine what the Terschelling bank would be like in a gale and no doubt it had claimed many bigger and stronger ships in its time than *Transcur*. The angry seas would crash down upon her with unbelievable force, the backwash sucking her bare like great vampires, until only her gaunt skeleton was left sticking out of the sand like a sentinel of misfortune. The mast would soon go, breaking away the deck planking as it toppled gracefully over and fell into the sea and her bowsprit would cock high up into the air as her back was broken and the lead ballast fell through her bottom onto the sand. The rudder would flail to and fro for no more than a few hours and then it would be wrenched away from the pintles and the rudder post would break off. Perhaps there would be a calm day and the beachcombers would come out and take what they could find. It would be a lucky day for them if they came across the pigs of lead ballast and were able to lift them and take them to the shore. Well, best of luck to them. Within a few months, or weeks if it blew hard, nothing would be left except the iron keel and the sand would soon close over it and make everything clean and smooth again.

I reached into my locker and took out my wallet with my money in it and looked round at all the familiar things, wondering if there was anything worth taking with me. It was almost dark now and if you didn't look at the water on the floor the cabin seemed homely and comfortable. The toys that Patrick and Adrian had been playing with when we first struck were on Celia's bunk, the tail of Anne's nightdress showed under the cushion at the head of her's—a ridiculous garment for a boat I had always considered that nightdress. The cabin lamp swung on its gimbals and every time *Transcur* pounded the sand the glass gave a little jump. Hanging to a nail on the mast were all

Transcur's and *Santa Lucia*'s trophies—souvenirs and badges from all the places we had been with the two boats—a tiny pair of castanets from Spain, a badge from Belle Isle, a pair of wooden clogs from our first trip to Holland in *Santa Lucia*. I took them off their nail and slipped them into my pocket, then I had second thoughts and put them back "Let them stay there—she might as well take them with her." I went out into the cockpit and took the life belt from its place round the rudder head and prepared to climb over the side into the sea. If I was going to go, better get away now before it was quite dark. Then I hesitated. "Maybe I'll just try with the engine once more."

I went into the cabin and pressed the self starter once again. The engine picked up at once and I put her into gear and stood by the throttle adjusting it as the seas swelled round the propeller. I could feel nothing except the endless pounding. I went out and looked ahead and in the dusk I could see the calmer water over the bow. It didn't look to me as if she was moving—in fact she was harder aground than ever she had been. Then I looked out to windward and saw a wave coming which was much bigger than the rest. It advanced like the side of a house and I could see that it was going to break just as it got to *Transcur*. It was a freak such as is occasionally seen in a big sea—one wave far bigger and more powerful than all the others. I stood by the throttle waiting for it to come and just as it began to lift *Transcur* I opened the throttle wide so that the engine roared like a racing car at the pits. When the wave hit *Transcur* heeled over and green water poured onto the cabin top and the deck, forcing itself through the sky lights and deluging into the cabin through the companionway. I had to hang on tight to the door post of Adrian's cabin as *Transcur* lifted and I waited in torment for the crash when she would fall back onto the sand. But she grounded very gently and when I went back into the cockpit I saw that she was moving ahead. She was still aground but now she was in deeper water and she was moving—inching ahead just as she had done before until with one last shattering crash onto the bottom and one last agonising convulsion she slid off the sand back into deep water.

73

Chapter Seven

There was a deep and satisfying luxury simply in being afloat, that I had never experienced before. The pounding, the banging and the nightmare shudders had gone and suddenly there was peace. I heard the cry of a gull as it wheeled into the dusk, and the steady music of the engine and the soft sweet lapping of the water against *Transcur*'s bow. It seemed to me that in all the time I had been sailing I had never been conscious of this exquisite tranquility before—this deep, gratifying peace. I was experiencing it all for the first time. Surely no evening before had ever been so lovely, no sea so calm and friendly, no breeze so caressing, moist and kindly and no old boat so strong and noble as this one? The tender harmonies of life had been restored and the whole of my little world was saturated with this longed for peace. "Thank the Lord Jesus Christ for that." To blaspheme is more of a nervous habit than a genuine conflict with one's own convictions, but on this occasion it was spoken right from the heart's core—it seemed to me something of a miracle that *Transcur* was afloat and more or less in one piece. Now, this small test of strength and resolution, although not yet over, had entered a more manageable phase.

In the past I have often sailed *Transcur* by myself, on short trips round about the Blackwater and occasionally on a passage

74

—I once sailed her across the Thames Estuary to Dover when I had no crew. Normally it is easy and pleasant enough, the thrill of being alone compensating for the lack of company. Over the years I have modified her gear in such a way that one person can manage her by himself without difficulty. Nothing is too heavy for one person to handle and no sail, with the exception of the big headsail, is too big or complicated for one person to be able to hoist or take in. Provided nothing goes wrong, common sense and reasonable strength are enough to take her along. But this time a great deal had gone wrong. She was half full of water and would have to be pumped out, there was an indescribable mess on deck and below which should be cleaned up, and in addition, I would have to navigate her in the dark, through an unfamiliar and narrow passage bounded by dangerous sands and complicated by a strong current, into a harbour of which I had no knowledge. But now I felt a rush of confidence and I was quite sure that I would have no difficulty in getting her into Terschelling—provided she could be kept afloat. Once there Celia and Anne would help me to find her a safe place to lie for the night and then we would see what had to be done. I expected that the boys would have been found a room in an hotel for the night and that they would be fast asleep by now. The time was eight thirty and I reckoned it would take me until ten thirty to get in. Celia and Anne and the boys had been ashore since just after seven and they should by now have had plenty of time to see that everything was ready for my arrival.

I steadied *Transcur* on what seemed a safe course and put a line round the tiller, adjusting it so that she would keep more or less straight. Then I went down to the cabin and hunted for the chart which had been bundled out of the way under the rubble of spare gear in the quarter berth. As I laid off the reverse course to the one we had been steering earlier—it seemed an age earlier—I glanced into the cabin and saw at once that the level of the bilge water had risen alarmingly. Then I set the course on the compass, adjusted the tiller lashings and went to work on the Vortex pump once more. The electric pump was foul with dirt from the bilge again and I cleaned this out and started it. The routine on the Vortex was slightly different now —twenty turns, then come up and look ahead to check that she was on course, then back for another twenty turns. The level of the water slowly began to go down. After the fourth stint of pumping I came up into the cockpit and saw dimly in the last of the light, the buoy at the end of the channel that we had passed going the other way, then I saw the lights and the outline of a small ship coming towards me. She was a small coaster and she came past not more than twenty yards away and circled once round *Transcur*. This, I thought, would be the assistance Celia had sent out from Terschelling. I stood up on the cockpit seats and leaning against the boom as casually as I could I waved at them in as calm a manner as I could muster and I could just see the three men standing on the bridge wave back. I supposed they must have had a radio message from the coast guard station at Terschelling and I thought to myself that they would be relieved not to have to embark on salvage or rescue operations just as night was coming on. I hoped they had not come out specially to find me but I thought it more likely that the coaster had been on her way out from Harlingen or Kornworderzand and had been sent a radio signal from the Terschelling lighthouse. I allowed myself a small smug feeling inside in the knowledge that I was not in need of help.

The coaster speeded up her engines again and with a last cheery wave she set off to the northward, away up the Thomas Smit Gat. I was astonished to see this. "God damn it, that's the channel that's closed." I went into the cabin, switched on the torch and checked it for the hundredth time on the chart. Sure enough, "Closed to navigation" is clearly written across the entrance to the Thomas Smit Gat. I came up and looked again at the coaster's stern light fast disappearing to the northward and I began to feel a deep sense of injustice. The Noordgat, which we had tried to use, appears from the chart to be a perfectly reasonable channel and it is mentioned without special comment in the North Sea Pilot—yet I now know that the Noordgat simply was not there. Seeing this coaster steam confidently away to the north through the Thomas Smit Gat made it quite clear that the normal channel lay that way and I had no doubt that it was buoyed right out to the edge of the Terschelling bank and that Celia and I had missed the buoys because of the poor visibility. In this case, I wondered indignantly, why was the chart marked "Closed to navigation"? What more could one do, I reflected, than buy the newest possible chart from the main Dutch Chart Depot and then follow it and put one's trust in it? I re-set the tiller lashing and went back to my pumping with the grievance rankling within me.

I was beginning to get tired and cold and hungry. I realised that I had eaten nothing since lunch time, surely a hundred years ago, in the lock at Kornworderzand. My clothes were wet and the heavy sea water made them cling to me, impeding movement and rubbing against me uncomfortably. It seemed that each of my bones was sending out its own individual signal of protest. "When the water goes under the floor, I'll change my clothes and when the pump sucks air I'll have something to eat." After each bout of pumping I went into the cockpit, checked the course and strained my eyes into the dark—thank God there would be a moon before long. I seemed to have lost the buoyed channel and now I could hear the surf rumbling to port so I altered the course a few degrees to starboard. I could see the big light on Terschelling sweeping a rhythmical finger round the horizon and I knew I had to find the red occulting light buoy at the entrance to the channel that leads up to the harbour. I was not sure how the tide would run in this entrance channel and I had no time to look it up in the pilot book. I pumped on in short snatches—twenty turns of the handle was as much as I could manage and after half an hour I cut it down to fifteen. The electric pump was drawing steadily and now that *Transcur* was on an even keel it no longer became blocked with grit. The engine kept steadily on, the water was going down and with one more big effort I could see in the dim light of the cabin that patches of floor board were drying off. I went out and looked again, listening to the rumble of the surf which I could still hear out to port. If I kept close to the surf on this side, surely I would have to pick up the light. Then I tore off my clothes, flung them

77

into the fo'c'sle and put on a dry shirt, dry trousers and one of Anne's sweaters that was lying on her bunk. This was real luxury. I found a bar of chocolate and stuffed it into my mouth.

The moon came up, the sky cleared, stars came out and now I could actually see the line of surf in the eerie light. I took out the lead and dropped it over, finding no more than one and a half fathoms—but who could ask for more than one and a half fathoms of water under the keel? The motor throbbed steadily on. "Bless its heart—may it keep right on going." But I knew we were steering a zig-zag course for every time I went below she would stray off one way or the other and then I would correct her when I came up from pumping the next time. In another twenty minutes the Vortex pump sucked air and the handle went limp in my hands. The electric pump I left running because it will take more water out of her than the Vortex, its rose lying right down in the bilge in the very bottom of the boat. I wondered whether she was leaking faster than the capacity of this electric pump but I thought that this was unlikely; if she had been, she would have foundered by now.

Now I was able to fix the floor board back in its position in the alleyway and this made the boat look civilized again and allowed me to walk into the cabin without gingerly treading on the bearers. I looked at the chart and hurriedly measured the distance to the buoy once again—it couldn't be more than three miles and I ought to see it now. Through the glasses I could see the line of the surf close to port and, in a moment, I saw one of the channel buoys on the other side, so that by altering to starboard I soon picked up three of them in a line and ran down beside them. We were back in the deep water channel and I knew we were on the correct course. "Now we're getting somewhere." Then, through the glasses, I clearly saw the red occulting light and a moment later I heard the electric pump sucking air and I knew the bilge was dry.

For some reason I don't understand, my mind went wheeling back again to that night in the life boat so many years ago and I remembered every detail of it with sparkling clarity. We had drifted aimlessly in the life boat for half an hour and then someone had seen a figure struggling weakly in the water and we had rowed the boat towards it. It was the engineer, probably within moments of the end of his life—coated with thick fuel oil so that at first I didn't know him for my friend. Somehow we managed to heave his oily bulk over the side of the life boat and we laid him out across one of the thwarts and did out best to clean the oil from his skin as he retched into the bottom of the boat. He had lost his glasses and seemed helpless like a blind puppy. The captain had taken off his white and gold jacket and his hat and folded them into a pillow. Then a red light shone clearly out of the night, like the light buoy at the entrance to the Terschelling channel, followed by the probing beam of a search-light which suddenly lit us all and showed us in all our confusion. The boat was crammed with men lying and sitting in all positions and in all states of dress and undress. The sea was a calm heaving lake of oil with odd pieces of wreckage and dunnage floating disconsolately on it. We heard the noise of diesel engines and in a moment the low bulk of a submarine was alongside us and a long boat hook gripped over our rail and pulled us close. A man with a machine gun in his hands stood on deck forward of the conning tower silhouetted against the moon and beside him a tall officer in shorts and peaked cap. "What ship Johnny?" No one answered. The man rattled the bolt of the gun and swept its muzzle expressively along the length of the boat. "Now you tell me what ship Johnny?" "Celtic Star" someone shouted from amidships. "Celtic Star." The officer was writing in a note book with the aid of a torch. "Where you from?" "Where you bound?" "What cargo?" The third mate was giving the answers while the rest of us were silent. "Where's your captain?" "He's gone down with the ship." "You officer?" "No, steward." We could see the crew in groups on the deck, talking in German among themselves, jumping up and down and clapping their hands over their heads for exercise. The man who was holding us alongside with the boat hook was pulling us hard against the bulging underwater hull of the submarine so that the wooden life boat was banging against the iron sides with heavy blows as the boat rose and fell on the swells—in a way, like *Transcur* hitting the hard

79

sand on the Terschelling bank. The officer looked up to a figure high above us at the top of the conning tower and the two held a conversation in German. Then the officer turned once more to us. "You want cigarettes?" "Yes." "Then you come on board I give you good German cigarettes." The third mate got up in the boat, stepped over the rail, grasped the officer's hand and was hauled on board the submarine. Then another man with a gun in his hand took him firmly by the arm, led him to a hatch and forced him down. The boat hook was taken from the rail and used to bear the life boat off from the submarine's side and suddenly there was a terrifying hiss as compressed air was released to start the diesel engines and the long black shape slipped away into the night, on the prowl for another sitting duck. None of us ever saw the third mate again.

Now that I had seen the buoy I knew that I was safe and that with a rising tide I would fetch Terschelling without too much trouble. I lit the navigation lights to be on the safe side in case there was traffic in the entrance channel and I counted the period of the light to make quite sure it was the right one. Soon I could see the next in the line of buoys that leads up to the harbour and the lights of the town itself shone clearly out making a friendly basin of light. I heard the surf again very loud out to port and took another sounding but this time the lead went down to five fathoms. Then *Transcur* came up to the buoy and I turned hard to port, bringing the town lights ahead. The tide was still with me and I realised that it must flow in a circular movement round the end of the island. I tried to square up the shambles on deck, making a neat stow of the mainsail and getting the fenders and the harbour ropes out ready for going alongside. Then I lifted the alleyway floor and saw that the bilge water was almost up to the level of the cabin sole again so I switched on the electric pump once more and checked that the discharge was flowing. Soon I could see the red and green lights on the harbour entrance and in another few moments I had turned to port again and was motoring through the entrance and up towards some ships that I saw lying alongside the quay. I looked out for Celia and Anne but no one was to be seen. It was eleven o'clock now and I realised that Terschelling along with every other Dutch town we had been to would already be fast asleep.

I suffered a sensation of anti-climax. I had expected Celia and Anne and possibly a coast guard or at least a couple of yachtsmen to whom she would have told her tale to be out waving and shouting at the end of the jetty and to be showing me where to bring *Transcur* alongside. I had thought that some sort of reception committee would have been waiting, eager to lend a helping hand—but evidently no one was interested. I had assumed without question that Celia would be safely in Terschelling and that it was she who had caused the coaster to come and look at me, but now for the first time I began to have glimmerings of doubt and to sense that something had gone wrong. Surely I had seen Celia and Anne and the boys safely ashore on the beach? Surely I could not have been mistaken?

Chapter Eight

Terschelling harbour is long and narrow with wooden staging against the shore constructed in successive "T's" so that the inside of the head of the "T" forms two basins where small boats can tie up. Coasters, the ferry to Harlingen and small ships tie up along the outside of the "T" so that there are, in effect, half a dozen different basins where yachts can moor. The seaward side of the harbour is formed by a detached mole which runs the whole length of it. I slowed the engine down and cruised the length of the harbour looking for a suitable entrance but as far as I could see each one was crammed with yachts and fishing boats and tugs and there did not seem to be any free space. When I got to the end the channel began to narrow and I carefully turned *Transcur* round in the centre of the stream and began to go back again.

I decided that I would just have to go in somewhere regardless of whether it was full or not and so I poked *Transcur*'s bowsprit as slowly and gently as I could into the second basin from the end. Yachts were moored on both sides but there was a space in the middle and it seemed that there would be room there for *Transcur* alongside a big motor boat flying the German ensign. I reversed the engine to take way off the boat and breasted alongside, *Transcur*'s bowsprit sticking out ahead of the German and just clear of a small Dutch yacht lying across the end of the basin. Suddenly a glass door in the motor boat's wheel house slipped back and a very fat man with a tiny peaked cap perched on his bald head appeared. He began to shout at me in German but I took no notice and threw him a rope which landed at his feet on the deck. Then he saw the red ensign at *Transcur*'s stern "No, no" he said in English "you cannot come here—there is no room. In any case" he said "your old boat will rub against my paint. No, no, go out again—go further along."

I left the cockpit and walked up the deck until I was opposite to where he was standing, and holding *Transcur* alongside by clutching the motor boat's rail. I said "Listen to me. Just listen for a moment. I am in some trouble. I have been on a sand bank and my boat is damaged. My wife and my children have been put ashore on a life raft and I must find them. Let me lie here until the morning and then I will shift." "No, no" he said "You can't lie here, you see there is not enough room. Your boat will brush against the sides of my yacht."

"Perhaps you did not hear what I said? I am in trouble. I must lie here until the morning." *Transcur* was already beginning to swing out so I stepped over onto his shining deck, took my bow line and made it fast to a chromium bollard on his bow. When I turned to go for the stern line—a strange figure I must have looked, untidy, unshaven and with Anne's much too small jersey on—the fat man had been joined by a thinner colleague and they stood threateningly in my way. "You cannot tie up here —if you are in trouble, go further down the harbour." I pushed roughly past them and went to get the other line which was coiled ready on *Transcur*'s stern. While I was there the thin man threw the bow line off the bollard and it snaked overboard and fell into the water.

Rage and frustration welled up inside me and I felt myself flushing and tingling with crude anger. "Right, you bastard" I muttered to myself "I'll teach you to mess me about." I was just stepping on board the motor boat again when I heard someone jump lightly onto *Transcur*'s deck behind me across the few feet that separated her from the yacht on the other side. A young

Dutchman, stocky and of medium height with a seaman's cap on the back of his head ducked under the boom and came up the deck towards me. "Leave this pork of a German to himself", he said to me quietly. "If you will put your engine astern, we will go into the next harbour and you can lie alongside my yacht". The Dutchman went to the tiller and put it over to starboard and I ran into the cabin and reversed the engine. "A little more speed please" he said. Then, "Steady her down". Then, "Neutral" as *Transcur* came comfortably stern first out from between the boats. "My name is Willem Smit. Slow ahead please", he said and *Transcur* gathered way again in a big circle, nosed into the next basin and came gently alongside a big Dutch boyer where two or three young men were standing ready to take her lines. Just as we tied up the electric pump began to suck air again.

As soon as we were safely tied up Willem came into the cabin and I saw a strong open face with clear blue eyes, wide apart, high cheek bones, a firm mouth and chin, and a muscular, supple physique. He looked tough, honest and sympathetic—above all sympathetic, the very person I wanted to meet at this moment. Willem looked round him at the shambles. "You are all alone?" he said. "Where is your crew? What trouble have you been in?" His English was extremely good with only the faintest accent and an occasional tendency to pick the wrong word. I told him what had happened as briefly and quickly as I could; his young cousin Jan came on board—his English was adequate but not quite so good as Willem's—and two other young men who were members of his family and who each spoke a little English. "You've been on the Noorder Grunden—that is a graveyard— you're lucky to be alive. Ships that go ashore there do not very often come off again. Your boat is strong" he said looking round at the solid oak frames showing in *Transcur's* cabin.

"Look Willem" I said, "you stay on board here and watch the pump while I go ashore and find out where Celia is. There is a big leak and the water is coming in almost as fast as the pump can take it out, but not quite. I'll switch on now and it will suck air again in about half an hour. Then you must switch it off so that it doesn't run dry—otherwise the impeller will burn out. And we shall have to pump by hand." I said "We" because I sensed in some strange way that Willem and I were in this together now. "All right" he replied. "While you are ashore I'll see if I can find where the water is coming in."

I climbed over the boyer, up onto the quay and walked along past the rows of brightly lit yachts lying alongside. As far as I could see none of them was English—they were mostly German and Dutch. The owner of a big Dutch cutter was standing on deck as I passed; I asked him where the Harbour Master's Office was and he directed me in good English to a square building near the quay. But there was no light to be seen in the window and no answer to my knock.

I walked slowly back towards *Transcur*, peering in at every yacht in case Celia and Anne should have gone aboard another boat and not known that I had arrived. As I passed the cutter again I told the owner that I had lost my wife and family but he seemed to regard me incredulously—thinking, perhaps, that I was another English eccentric—and suggested that they were staying in an hotel in another part of the island. But I knew Celia was not staying in any hotel. On my way back to *Transcur* I stopped every person I met and if he spoke English I explained my predicament, asked him where the Harbour Master could be found, and made him promise to come and tell me if he heard anything of two English girls and two small children.

There seemed to be some mystery about the nocturnal habits of the Harbour Master who ought by all accounts to have been in his little square house but who had melted into the night air. It was getting late and already the lights in the yachts were going out and only a few people were to be seen on the quay. I went back on board *Transcur*, puzzled and undecided what to do. I knew that if I did not act soon the whole town would be asleep and then it would be a very difficult matter to rouse the solid Dutch out of their beds. In *Transcur* Willem had the floor boards up, the mattress and all the loose gear from Anne's bunk was piled in a big heap on Celia's bunk together with spare rope, tackles, paint, blocks, flares, coils of wire, rigging screws and the

85

entire miscellaneous contents of the big locker under Anne's bunk. Willem was taking out the wooden floor of the locker. "I think I have found the leak" he said in triumph. Jan was standing by the electric pump and Willem's father, Mr. Smit, was directing the proceedings. It was quite clear that the whole operation had been taken out of my hands and that, if anything, I was in the way.

"Go on board the boyer" Mr. Smit said to me, "and my wife will give you coffee." The boyer's cabin was warm and supremely comfortable in the pleasant untidy sort of way that makes a boat's cabin into a home. I recognised it at once as a haven of calm. Mrs. Smit and her sister knew all about my troubles and gave me steaming hot and quite superb coffee, with some sort of homemade shortbread biscuits which tasted delectable. They both spoke competent English and asked anxiously about Celia and Anne and the children. "I'm really worried about them now" I said, "I think I will ask your husband if he will come with me to the police or the coastguards. Otherwise I shall never make myself understood." On board *Transcur* Willem and Mr. Smit had their heads in the locker under Anne's bunk and I looked over their shoulders to see the water bubbling up between two of her frames and running fast into the bilge. Willem said "Have you got some—how do you say it—stuffing?" "Caulking cotton—yes I have—but you'll never stop that leak from the inside." The leak was under the cement in the bilges and I knew that as fast as they stopped it from coming in in one place the water would find another. But Willem was sure that he could at least improve the leak and I gave him a ball of caulking cotton and told him to be careful not to use it all up. Then a voice shouted out in Dutch from the shore and Mr. Smit held a brief shouted conversation. "There's a man on shore, a German, who says your wife and family are safe in an hotel and if you will come ashore he will take you to them."

I felt a great flood of relief but it was mixed with puzzlement. What on earth was Celia doing in an hotel? I wondered. Maybe for some reason she was unable to leave the children—or perhaps they had met with some accident. I paused to change my shoes and put on a jacket, and then on my way across the boyer to the shore I slid open the hatch and said to Mrs. Smit, "I think they're found." She replied "Let the children sleep on board here tonight if they would like to." I walked ashore but to my astonishment there was no one to be seen. I ran along the quay for a few yards but still I could find no one. Puzzled, I ran the other way but there was not a soul to be seen—it was nearly midnight now and the town was fast asleep. The lights in the houses were almost all out and the boats were dark. The mysterious messenger had evaporated into the night. I went back to Mr. Smit "This man has gone—there's no sign of him. You must come with me to the police."

"What? He is not there? This is extraordinary." Mr. Smit came ashore with me and we conferred with a friend of his from another boat in the harbour. There was no sign of the unknown messenger and Mr. Smit did not know who it had been. "We will walk to the police house" he said and we all three set off up through the village. By now I was frantic with worry. "We must go faster." There was a light in the policeman's house and his wife came bustling to the door in answer to our knock and then there was a long conversation which I could not understand. After an endless delay Mr. Smit told me that the policeman was out and when he was not there the telephone was switched through so that it could not be used from the house. Apparently it was not possible to tell where the policeman was to be found, neither could we communicate from his house. The policeman's wife said she was sorry and closed the door.

I said to Mr. Smit "This is now very serious. We must at once get to a telephone and raise the alarm." But Mr. Smit was calmer than I—in fact he was so calm that I began to doubt whether he really believed in the existence of Celia and Anne and Patrick and Adrian—the whole experience was becoming an endlessly confused nightmare and I myself began to doubt things which I knew to be true, particularly that I had seen Celia and Anne and the boys walking up the beach on the far side of the island. The more agitated I became the more calm was Mr. Smit. It seemed impossible to rouse him to any sense of an emergency. I was beginning to understand something of the character of these people who had built their country sod by sod out of nothing—so innured to the constant battle with forces vastly stronger than themselves that the normal emergencies of everyday life left them unmoved. At length it was agreed that Mr. Smit's friend should telephone to every hotel in the island and if no clue was unearthed, to the coast guards and the life boat station. Mr. Smit and I would go back to *Transcur*.

Willem was still trying to mend the leak. He was forcing the caulking cotton into every crack that showed water but as fast as one place was stopped the water bubbled through in another. If anything, he had made the leak slightly worse by scraping cement away from the inside of the hull and now the electric pump, still watched by Jan, was running almost continuously. I wondered for how long the pump could possibly run without developing a fault and Willem and I tried to estimate the life of the 12 volt battery with a constant discharge of five amps. We thought it would probably run all night provided the pump did not break down and we decided that if necessary we would run the engine to recharge. It would be back-breaking work keeping *Transcur* afloat without the electric pump and I thought with a shudder of the prospect of winding the Vortex almost continuously for the remainder of the night. Willem and Jan and their two cousins had succeeded in making a tremendous mess in the cabin. The pile of gear on Celia's bunk was by now monumental, a great mound of our possessions looking rather pathetic when piled up haphazardly. The whole of the cabin floor was up and the boards were pushed to one side so that to walk through the cabin you had to step gingerly on the bearers. One of Anne's brassieres and a pair of frilly pants perched ridiculously on top of the mound, suggesting a depravity of which we were innocent. The cabin looked like a whore's garret after a night's debauch.

"If it wasn't that I know I saw them land on the beach", I said to Willem, "I would have raised much more of a fuss and I would have made sure that a full scale search had been started, even if everyone is asleep. Then that German chap and his message. What do you make of that? Why would anyone come with a story like that if it were not true? And why in God's name, didn't he wait for me to come ashore?" The thought flashed across my mind that perhaps the German motor boat owner had put the story out for the purpose of revenging himself. It is true that I had been rude to him but I had done him no real injury—thanks to Willem's arrival at the right moment.

"How long will your friend be with his telephoning?" I asked Mr. Smit. "No more than a few minutes. He has to go to the house of a friend and ask to use the telephone. It's late now." Mr. Smit looked at his watch, "After midnight and his friend will have to be got out of bed." It was just possible, I supposed that Celia and Anne and the children were in some hotel and had sent a message to me that had not arrived but this was so uncharacteristic of both of them that I could not credit it unless they had been overtaken by some accident. I found myself quite unable to take any constructive part in Willem's efforts to stop *Transcur*'s leak further than to tell him yet again that he would never be able to stop it from the inside. At least we knew where the leak was, and once Celia turned up we would be able to make some plan for mending it. I went back to Mrs. Smit in the boyer, had some more coffee and thrashed the whole thing through with her and Mr. Smit yet again while we waited for a tread on the deck that would be Mr. Smit's friend with a telephone message. Waiting in anxiety tears the nerves to shreds and I wanted desperately to be doing something. Some people have reserves of calm that enable them to stand this kind of strain but any composure that I might in normal circumstances have been able to muster, had been destroyed by the harrowing events of the day. "I'm going ashore to have another look down the quay."

All was quiet and peaceful now. The moon was high among the stars, throwing its soft light over the harbour so that masts and derricks and funnels stood up in a jagged line against the sea beyond the mole. There were lights in a few boats and voices carried across the water in a jumble of unfamiliar language. A boy and his girl hurried along the quay and up into the town on some errand but otherwise there was no movement except

89

the gentle rustle of water against the harbour wall. I walked to the end of the quay yet again and saw nothing. "I'll walk back to the boyer, and if nothing has happened by the time I get there, I'll raise hell and wake this town up." I reproached myself for not having acted as soon as I had got into the harbour. Hours had been wasted because I had been fooled by vague messages and bogus reassurances and all the time Celia and Anne and the boys were probably in some dire trouble. I hurried back along the quay resolved to make a big fuss and arrived at the boyer at the same time as Mr. Smit's friend.

We went together into the cabin. He reported his findings to Mr. Smit in Dutch and I had to wait, it seemed interminably, for the explanation. "Our friend has telephoned to every hotel in the island", he told me "No one knows anything about your wife except one man who said that two women with children had asked for a room for the night, but he was full and turned them away."

"All right," I said to Mr. Smit "it is now half past twelve. You must come with me at once to the coastguards and we must raise the alarm. The beaches and the foreshore of this island must be searched. We cannot delay any longer." "Yes," Mr. Smit replied "you're right, we will go now."

The three of us went ashore and walked along the quay to the right. When we had gone a hundred yards the road forked sharp left away from the harbour and as we turned to walk up this road I heard it.

"Just a minute," I said to Mr. Smit. "Listen." I heard Patrick's voice ringing out clear as a bell through the night. There is no mistaking a child's high pitched, excited voice and this time it was the most exquisite sound I had ever heard—clearer and finer than the Queen of the Night. "Mummy, I can see Transcur's mast. I know I can see it Mummy, look it's there. It is Transcur's mast Mummy."

90

Chapter Nine

Celia had weathered many crises in our sailing experiences but leaving *Transcur* on the Terschelling bank, in a life raft with the children, takes pride of place for being the most unpleasant and nerve racking. It had never really occurred to her, or for that matter to me, that the life raft would ever be used in anger by any of us. Although when it had been bought, Celia had insisted that it was for the safety of the children, she had never really believed that we would actually use it. It was there, simply for an emergency, but she never considered that the emergency would involve us personally. We had thought that the life raft would be useful if we came across some other boat in difficulties—or in any number of unspecified circumstances. But Celia knew that things had a habit of happening to her for the first time—things that she thought could not happen; since we have been sailing together there have been enough alarms and near disasters to convince her of that. She had never thought that she and I would find ourselves caught in a gale in the Bay of Biscay in a boat only eighteen feet long that leaked heartily. Neither had she foreseen that *Santa Lucia* could have been trapped by a steamer in a Dutch lock and crushed against a stone wall. Nor had it seemed likely to her that we should find ourselves tied alongside an exposed harbour wall in the Wash in a northerly gale so that *Transcur* shook and banged until we were all almost insensible. When all these things happened to her they left her with a feeling of hurt surprise but every time she was ready and willing to face the next experience. She is made of resilient material.

The moment she jumped into the life raft it was borne away on a wild, snarling sea and she looked up to see *Transcur*'s bowsprit-end sail past the opening in the canopy so that she thought she was already adrift. It wasn't until the raft swung round so that she could see *Transcur* through the opening in the canopy that she realised that I was laboriously pulling her back alongside with the painter. The raft was already full of water and an assortment of gear was floating about in the bottom of it—her own small zip bag in which she had packed her hastily contrived kit of essentials was already under water and two other bags of spare gear supplied with the raft were floating from side to side. The rubber floor was soft yet quite firm and the inflated sides with the canopy behind them were hard to the touch. As I pulled it back alongside she saw that the raft was obviously a stable and seaworthy craft and she did not fear for the children's safety in it. She thought it would be easy enough to bale out the water once they were all in it and, in any case, it was obvious that being water-logged did not impede the raft's stability. It was not a craft she would have chosen to spend the afternoon in with the children but it was better than staying in *Transcur* and having her break to pieces round them. If only everybody was coming off in the raft it would be better.

Patrick was the first to join her and was at once bundled to the back where he squatted down on the bottom with the water swilling round his legs and his trousers. Then Anne came in neatly enough. Adrian was the last and as the raft rose to a sea she saw me take hold of him and begin to pass him over *Transcur*'s rail. She wanted to tell me to wait because she could see that the next wave was much bigger than the others, rising up behind my back and out of my sight. But it was too late, I was already holding Adrian out for her to grasp him. The wave hit him just as he was between *Transcur* and the raft. She had her two hands round his waist when a solid wall of water engulfed them both and threatened to convey her and Adrian right out of the raft. The water seemed to engulf her and poured solid over her, turning everything a pale green colour and making Adrian's small frame into an intolerable weight which pressed her arms downwards towards the sea. Then, just as she thought he would be washed away from her, the pressure of the water began to ease and she was able to pass him through the opening in the canopy. Adrian was silent, his little face set and grim as he squatted down in the water beside Patrick. "Mummy it's jolly wet in this raft" Patrick said "Can we bale it out?" "Yes we will as soon as we get clear of Transcur" Anne answered for Celia. Celia caught my eye for the last time before she was set adrift, with an expression of unimpeded tenderness "Good luck."

"Now boys, we shall soon be ashore" she said "We'll get some of this water out first." She and Anne looked round for the bailer which she knew should be in the raft. There was a polythene bag with the bailer in it tied up with boat lacing, but the knot in the lacing had shrunk tight and neither of them could undo it. Anne said "I meant to bring my knife but I left it on board." Celia found her handbag which she had put out of the bilge water on the side of the raft and searched in it for a little pair of folding nail scissors that she always carries. She found the scissors and gave the handbag to Patrick "Listen Pad, you look after my bag and keep it dry for me." While Celia and Anne struggled with the knot Patrick managed to tuck the handbag close up under the canopy where it was dry. He managed to squeeze himself up onto the side as well, pushing his back against the canopy so that he could get his bottom out of the water. Now the raft was well clear of *Transcur* and was moving into the roughest part of the surf. The waves hissed and roared round them but the raft kept level and stable. It was turning slowly round and round and every time the opening in the canopy faced the wind, a wave would wash in over the side so that it was quite full of water.

At last, Anne managed to cut the lacing on the bag and they took out a selection of flares and a repair kit in case the raft

93

should spring a leak, and the bailer. Celia started to shovel water out through the opening. Adrian was beginning to shiver with the cold and to whimper quietly to himself and Celia passed the bailer to Anne and turned to comfort him "You'll be all right old chap" she said to him soothingly. She pulled up out of the water the small suitcase which they had brought with them, up-ended it and seated Adrian on it so that he was out of the water except for his feet and was able to lean back against the canopy beside Patrick. He stopped whimpering at once when he was out of the water and more comfortable. Patrick said "Mummy, where's Daddy. Is he all right? Can you see him?"

Anne glanced up towards *Transcur* as the opening swung round. The trim yacht that she knew so well was a sorry sight now, heeling over on her side; the movement that was shaking the guts out of her was hardly perceptible to Anne—*Transcur* seemed to be heaving and jerking herself in spasms like a wounded animal striving with its last breath to regain its feet. She could see the sails lying in a jumble about the deck and a rope's end streaming out on the wind from the top of the mast. The boom was lying over the side, the end of it washed by the surf. It looked as though everything on board was chaos and confusion instead of the rigorous sense of order that had always struck Anne when she saw *Transcur* from a distance. To add to this dejection great columns of water would leap into the air round her stern when a wave struck her transom. "Daddy's fine", she lied to Patrick, "he's standing up in the cockpit, lean-ing on the boom and smoking his pipe." Between bailing, Celia was looking round the raft for paddles which she felt sure would be on board somewhere but although there was a collection of flares and the leak stopping gear and a torch, all swilling in the water, there were no paddles to be seen. "I could have sworn Frank said there were paddles on board" she muttered. Anne was leaning through the opening paddling with her hands to keep the opening turned away from the seas so that more water could not come in. After a few minutes bailing they began to make an impression and the level of the bilge in the raft went down.

When they had been baling for ten minutes and the raft began to be less waterlogged, Celia paused in her labours, put her head through the opening and looked about her. It was a wild white world that she saw, with the breaking surf all around them. There was no rhythm or order in the way the seas were running and they broke in every direction, sending spray over the raft and crashing against the back of the canopy with a hollow noise; for all that the raft was surprisingly steady. In front of her was the line of the shore but she perceived with dismay that instead of being blown towards it by the wind they were in the grip of the tide which was taking them along parallel to the beach. Then she saw to her left a point of land and beyond it the line of the beach turned sharply to the south and there was nothing but the open sea.

"Anne, do you see that?", she said urgently, "If we get carried past that point we shan't get ashore at all—we'll be carried right out to sea. Look, we'll have to start paddling as best we can with our hands and the bailer. We haven't got far to go, but if we miss that point we shall be in trouble." They both settled themselves in the opening, kneeling side by side in the bilge water and leaning out over the sea, Celia to the left and Anne to the right. Celia used the bailer with her left hand and Anne used both her hands to paddle with, stretching her arms out as far as possible, grasping at the water with cupped hands and trying to pull the raft sideways with it. They worked together in a steady rhythm—stretching out and pulling towards them over and over again until it seemed that this motion would go on for ever like a torture in some grotesque dream of after-life. The boys sat side by side behind them in the back of the raft, Adrian silent but Patrick keeping up a steady stream of quite cheerful conversation that did not seem to require any answer. Patrick always talks a lot, mostly as a relief from nervous excitement.

After half an hour's paddling they stopped and surveyed their progress. The beach was nearer and they were out of the worst of the surf now. *Transcur* was away to windward, shrouded in mist so that sometimes they could see her and sometimes they

95

could not. "One more spell" Anne said, "and we'll be near enough to get ashore. Come on." They settled to their work again and now that they were clear of the surf they could see that they were not going to be carried past the point. The battering of the waves on the outside of the canopy had stopped and the raft was quieter. The tide seemed to be a little less strong as they got closer to the shore. In another twenty minutes they were really close to the point and a few yards on the right side of it. "I'm sure I could stand here" Anne said "I'm going to try." She turned round so that the top part of her body was inside the raft and lowered her legs over the side feeling for the bottom with her feet as the water came up to her waist. Then she touched the firm hard sand. "Hurrah" Celia cried "We're there." "Well done Cousin Anne" Patrick shouted. Anne took a few steps towards the shore, pulling the raft behind her, then suddenly her foot went into a depression in the sand and she slipped and fell in the water up to her neck. "Oh well" she spluttered, "I was half wet and now I'm all wet. I don't suppose it makes much difference." Celia smiled to herself as she thought of the language that would have occurred if a similar thing had happened to me. Anne pulled the raft after her towards the shore until it grounded gently on the beach.

Celia got out of the raft and between them she and Anne pulled it a few feet up onto the beach. "We'll have to get the water out of it, otherwise we'll never manage to pull it." The boys scrambled out onto the shore. "Now run about as fast as you can and get warm. Go and explore round and find the best way for us to get up to the sea wall." They were all stiff and cold as well as wet after being cramped up in the raft. Celia guessed the time at about eight o'clock and it was beginning to be dusk. She looked round for *Transcur* and saw her appearing and disappearing as the mist swirled round her. It looked a desolate beach and it was a good way to where the flat sand gave way to low dunes, apparently covered with coarse grass; about a mile, she thought. Anyway, once they had got across the sand there was certain to be a house or a farm where they would be able to ask for help. Holland, she reflected, was like a garden and you never had to go for more than a few yards before you stumbled on someone or something.

She and Anne unloaded the gear from the raft and made a pile of it on the beach. The small suitcase, small zipper bag and the polythene envelopes with the life raft gear in them. Then they managed to heave the raft up on its side and empty the water out of it. "You carry the gear Anne, and I'll tow the raft across the sand." They all set off up the beach, Anne and the children on ahead with the gear and Celia behind, pulling the raft across the sand by its painter. The raft was heavy and progress was slow. She held the painter over her shoulder but the thin rope cut into her skin, she tried fastening it round her waist but this made it uncomfortable, almost impossible, to walk; she tried pulling the raft along by the life lines round the side of it but although this was easier, she had to stoop down to grasp the lines and her back began to ache. After they had been going for less than a quarter of a mile they came to a long narrow strip of water in their way, a sort of low tide lagoon, parallel to the sea and immediately in front of them.

"Can we wade across it?" Anne said. "I don't know, it looks deep. Why don't you walk round the end of it with the children and I'll launch the raft and try to paddle across." The boys and Anne set off to skirt the lagoon to the west and Celia tried to launch the raft; but the sides of the lagoon were steep and she suddenly stepped off the hard sand into deep mud, missed her balance, fell and had to drag herself out onto the sand again. She tried to launch the raft once more in another spot further along the edge of the lagoon but again she slipped into mud. She looked up and saw that Anne and the children were already some way off and so she shouted after them "Anne, Anne!" After two more shouts they heard her and she saw them pause and turn. "Wait for me. I'm going to leave the raft" she shouted.

It was the only possible thing to do. It would be mad to try and drag the raft right round the end of the lagoon—it was too heavy and she knew she would never manage it. With every step the raft became heavier and more awkward and she was already exhausted with the effort of dragging its bulk across the sand.

97

She looked round for a stone or anything heavy to tie the raft on to but there was nothing but the endless expanse of fine sand and so, reluctantly, she just left the painter lying loose. "Oh well, you'll have to look after yourself. Maybe someone will find you tomorrow." She began to hurry after the others. It was hard going, trying to hurry in the sand which was much softer here, although it was a blessed relief to be rid of the weight of the raft. The sand seemed to cling to her feet so that it was impossible to run more than a few steps—the more you try to hurry in soft sand the heavier and more tiresome it becomes. She caught up with them breathlessly and as she came near them she began to realise for the first time that her leg was beginning to hurt again. "I had to leave it. I couldn't launch it and it's too heavy to pull." They were at the end of the lagoon and they all took one last look out to sea towards *Transcur* before striking inland. At first they couldn't see her but then the mist rolled away for an instant and she came into view. "She's off the sand, she's under way" Patrick shouted.

Celia was not so sure as Patrick that *Transcur* was, in fact, off the sand, but she said, "Well, that's a blessing. Thank God for that." Certainly *Transcur* had appeared to be afloat in the brief moment in which she had been visible, but Celia thought she had seen the boat lurch violently the second the mist closed in again. "I wonder" she muttered under her breath.

It was easier now that they had left the life raft behind but it was clear that it was going to be a long walk before they passed over the sand dunes. After half an hour's tramping laboriously through the sand they abandoned the little leather suitcase and a pair of trousers belonging to me which Celia had brought with them in an excess of wifely zeal. All the spare gear for the life raft, including the flares, were left on the sand. This made it easier, but they were all getting tired. The boys were suffering from their wet trousers chafing against their legs and it was impossible for them to walk fast on the soft sand. Anne's clothes were drying off but she was getting tired as well; Celia's bad leg was a constant and wearing reminder of pain.

They had been in a high state of nerves when they had packed the gear they were to take with them and the resulting choice had been dictated more by what had first come into their heads than by considered logic. Adrian had perhaps been the most composed. "I won't take my bear", he had said to Celia "because I really think he's too old and frail for this sort of journey. I'll take Spot-on-the-Bumble." This last animal is a dog, given him by Anne when he was a baby, and curiously named from Adrian's boundless imagination. Patrick, on the other hand, had decided that his bear should share any adventures equally with himself and both these animals underwent the journey tucked behind the zips in the boys' jackets. Celia had packed cigarettes, the bottle of brandy and another bottle with some water in it, all our passports, some chocolate, her money and the spare pair of trousers now abandoned. She had left a good bit more chocolate and dry clothes on board. Anne had forgotten her knife in the excitment of leaving *Transcur* although it is provided with a lanyard and had been given her by me on a previous cruise specifically for some such emergency.

At last they reached the bottom of the first sand dune and clambered to the top on hands and knees. But instead of the civilized landscape they had expected, there was only an endless expanse of sand undisturbed by a road or dwelling or any sign of habitation, and interspersed with low sand hills, stretching away into the distance as far as they could see. Ahead of them, it seemed endless miles away, was the winking lighthouse at Terschelling showing up clearly in the gathering night.

Celia and Anne gazed with astonishment at the view before them but they were careful not to say anything that might alarm the children. They exchanged a look that carried dismay from one to the other. For a moment they were silent, Anne holding Adrian's hand and Celia Patrick's, standing in a group on top of the hillock and surveying in the last of the daylight a wilderness of sand before them, a wilderness of sea behind them and no relieving features except the rhythmic blink of the lighthouse far away. Then Celia said "I think we'd better start walking round the beach this way" pointing to the west, "until we find a road or a path that leads towards the lighthouse." They set off in pairs, each boy holding a reassuring hand, along the top of the beach at the foot of the sand hills. They walked steadily, not too fast but fast enough to cover a reasonable amount of ground, until Anne saw what looked like the marks of a motor tyre in the sand. Celia found the life raft's torch which she had in her zip bag and they identified the wheel marks as those of a car or a truck and followed them for a quarter of an hour. Then the marks turned inland and passed through a gap in the sand hills; they turned with them but soon the marks seemed to become indistinct and finally they could no longer see them even with the light from the torch. The torch had been soaked with water and was flickering on and off so that it was not very much help. Celia said "I think we'll stop and have a rest. Come on, there's a patch of grass over there."

They all sat down in a circle and Celia took out chocolate and gave a piece to each boy. She found a packet of biscuits in her bag but they were soaked in sea water and inedible. "Oh well," she said, "we'll all have a drink." She opened the bottle of brandy and poured some for Patrick using the top of the lemonade bottle in which she had brought water as a cup. Patrick put his head back and swallowed the brandy in one gulp and the cup was filled and passed to Adrian. He took a sip and spluttered "Mummy, it's very fiery stuff", but he too managed to drink the bottle top full. Celia and Anne each had a swig out of the bottle. The boys lay down in the sand and in one moment they were both fast asleep. Celia found a more or less dry packet among the cigarettes she had brought and she started striking the damp matches until one suddenly flared up and she lit it. She passed a cigarette to Anne and lit it for her from her own and then they both sat and puffed for a few minutes. Celia said "We mustn't stay here too long. The boys will have to be woken up before they get cold and we'll get cold too if we sit here for too long".

Anne lay down on the short coarse grass. "I'm going to have a sleep for a minute" she said. Celia sat with her knees hugged up under her chin looking at the night, at the moon coming up and the stars which had all come out, and puffed at her cigarette. When it was finished she lit another from it. They would just have to press on towards the lighthouse, she thought, and surely they must come across a road or at least a path leading towards Terschelling.

She glanced down at the boys lying side by side. It was hours past their bed time and the brandy had finished them off. All the same, she knew she must not go to sleep because if she did, she might not wake for two or three hours, by which time it would be midnight and then it would be the devil of a job to get everyone moving again. Added to that, if *Transcur* was off the sand, she would be back in Terschelling before then and if they were too long there would be search parties and God knows what else out after them. She finished her cigarette and put a hand on Patrick's shoulder and shook him gently "Come on old chap. We must be on our way." Then she roused Adrian and both the boys stood up, blinking and yawning and striving to discover where they were and what this adventure in the middle of the night was all about. "Mummy, is this a desert island?" Adrian asked her sleepily. "Well not exactly a desert island, although there is a lot of sand about." "Well, Mummy, are there lions on this island?" "No darling, I promise you there are no lions or tigers."

They pulled themselves together and set off again towards the lighthouse. Celia didn't really remember exactly where the lighthouse was situated but she thought she had seen on the chart that it was in the town, or village, of Terschelling. "Anyway we must make for the lighthouse because that's the only thing we can see" she remarked to Anne with simple logic. She and Anne sorted through the gear that was left, abandoned a good bit more of it and separated the remainder into two equal loads which they shared between them. Now they walked faster than before because the chill of the summer's night was already eating into them so that it was essential to get some briskness into their circulations. Celia had half expected the boys to whine and complain when they were woken up but they walked on steadfastly and without complaint, conserving their energy for the business of making progress. They walked across ground still sandy with patches of grass and scrub showing black against the light colour of the sand in grotesque shapes and outlines. There was still no sign of a track or path but after the best part of an hour's walking they began to see lights in front of them when they came to the tops of the hillocks.

"There" Anne said, "It can't be so much further now." The boys began to get very tired and to show signs of lagging back. Patrick's hand was clasped firmly round Celia's fingers and his warm firm grip was sending pulsations of strength into her that made her forget the pain in her leg. Then they came to a track running at right angles to their path. They paused, wondering whether they should walk to the right or to the left and after some discussion they set off to the right. But they had chosen wrongly and in another ten minutes the track turned sharply away from the lighthouse and back towards the sea. "We'll have to go back" Celia said "this is obviously wrong." They turned and retraced their steps; they made up the ground they had lost and then the track veered round towards the lights. "Time for another rest" Anne said.

They all sat down on another patch of grass and Celia poured out another mouthful of brandy for each boy. She managed to find a dry cigarette and to light it. Patrick said, "Mummy, where are we going to sleep tonight? Surely we can't lie down and sleep out here?" "When we get to Terschelling I expect Transcur will be there", Celia replied "and we shall sleep on board". "And suppose Transcur isn't there?" he pursued. "Then we shall have to find a hotel and sleep there I suppose." "I do hope we can sleep in our own bunks" Adrian said wearily. "Come on," Anne said, "one more real try and we shall be there." They shared out the last of the chocolate between the two boys and continued again along the path, fortified by the brandy, each boy clinging firmly to a hand. The ground was getting more hilly and the scrub was giving way to pine woods that came right down to the edge of the path. They could see the lights of the town clearly now and in another half an hour they had reached the first houses. Then they passed round the base of the huge lighthouse tower and could see the quay in front of them with the

102

lines of moored boats; there was nobody to be seen. First they walked along the quay to the west, Patrick and Celia looking in vain at every boat and every mast until they came to the end of the quay. They peered through the dark across the harbour wall and out past the entrance but still there was nothing familiar to be seen.

"We'll try the other end now" Celia said as cheerfully as she could. She had a sick, empty feeling in her stomach, her head was beginning to split with worry and her bones ached. "I know Transcur's going to be here" Patrick was saying with a note of desperation in his voice, "I know she's here. I know she's here. I know she's here." They retraced their steps and began to walk to the other end of the quay, scrutinising every boat in the dim light as they went by. Patrick ran on ahead and Celia heard him shouting excitedly but by now she was convinced inside herself that his endless optimism was carrying him away on a fantasy, as it always did. She suddenly felt that she was descending into a gloomy chasm. There would be more decisions to be made, arrangements, plans, explanations—she felt so tired in her brain and her body that she wondered where she would get the strength to live through the next few hours. She only wanted to be in bed somewhere, safe and asleep. Then she saw me and Mr. Smit running along the quay towards her and suddenly, on an upsurge of elation, she forgot she had ever been tired as the relief flooded into every pore of her being, flushing away her anguish.

Chapter Ten

Patrick clasped me round the waist. "Hello Daddy" he said, "hello Daddy, how's Transcur? Is she all right? Can I go on board?" "Yes Transcur's fine, she's leaking a bit but she's fine." "I'm going on board", he said and he jumped aboard the boyer and ran across her deck to where *Transcur* was lying. Adrian said, "Hello Daddy, we have had a long walk." He was asleep on his feet and it was all he could do to make any comment at all. Celia and I exchanged our stories in brief, disjointed sentences, using the kind of verbal shorthand which people who know one another very well often use—a composite language made up of looks, expressions and a few words so that meanings and feelings are conveyed in split seconds. Anne said, "I don't think I've ever been more pleased to see anyone in my life." We all went with Mr. Smit into the warm homely cabin of the boyer and Mrs. Smit had cups of hot delicious coffee in Celia's and Anne's hands almost before they had sat down, and was pressing shortbread biscuits on them.

Everybody talked at once in a welter of relief at the sudden lifting of anxiety, like people in an air raid shelter who have heard the flying bomb pass safely overhead—everyone, that is, except Adrian who was asleep on Celia's lap, Spot-on-the-Bumble leering amiably over the zip of his jacket. Mrs. Smit said "I think your boys should sleep here tonight. We have plenty of beds" and Celia agreed with her. After a few minutes I went across to *Transcur* to bring Patrick back on board the boyer. He was standing athwart the floor bearers in the cabin in deep conversation with Willem and Jan who were still trying to stem the leak with caulking cotton. "You can't stop leaks from the inside", he was saying to Willem, "She'll have to go up on the slip to have that job done." I butted in, Willem smiled good humouredly at Patrick. "Listen Patrick, go on board the boyer and Mrs. Smit will give you a drink of warm milk. You and Adrian are going to sleep on Mr. Smit's boat tonight while we get things sorted out on Transcur." "Daddy, I want to sleep in my own bunk in Transcur" he said firmly and no amount of argument could persuade him to change his mind. We went back to the boyer. Celia had just woken Adrian and he was saying to her, "But Mummy, I don't want to sleep on this boat. I want to sleep in my own bunk, in Transcur." Celia and Anne brought the boys back on board *Transcur* and somehow among the mess they were found clean pyjamas and put to bed, each in his rightful place. They snuggled down into their own sleeping bags luxurious as we kissed them good night and closed the fo'c'sle door and Adrian's door. They were asleep in seconds, content enough with their day of high adventure. "They won't forget that for a long time" Celia said.

We all went back on board the boyer leaving Jan to watch the pump in *Transcur* and leaving the mess to be cleaned up later. "Come and have a glass of gin with us" Mr. Smit said, "While we decide what must be done." It was obvious that *Transcur* would have to be put on a slip, or at least beached, without delay. We were dependent on the electric pump which had already been running more or less continuously for upwards of seven hours and, in the nature of things, it could not be expected to go on for much longer. If it stopped we should have to pump by hand, which would be laborious as well as inconvenient. The next low tide would be at half past seven in the morning and she ought to be beached not later than four a.m. to allow the water to leave her sufficiently for a temporary repair to be made before the water came up again at the next tide. Willem said that there was a small slip in Terschelling, just near where we were lying, but he was not sure whether it was in working order or not and whether it could take a boat of *Transcur's* size. In any case, we would not be able to organise the slip in the night ready for the early tide and so she would have to be beached first. Willem thought he could find for me two pieces of stout timber about eight feet long to make sheer-legs of, and he and I went ashore straight away to where there was a pile of timber lying on the quay. "We'll borrow two of these" he said and we selected two excellent sheer-legs and carried them on board *Transcur*, laying them along the decks one on each side. He pointed up the harbour beyond the end of the mole and said "There is a spot there which should serve well. We'll put her on at four in the morning." It was arranged that he and Jan and the rest of his family should go to bed and that I should wake them at four so that they could come with me and help me put *Transcur* on the beach. Celia and I were diffident about asking so much of them all, but Mr. Smit waved our objections to one side, "Of course we will help you" he said, "It is good for these boys to have something to do with themselves."

It was agreed that I should call Willem and Jan and the various Smit cousins at quarter to four in the morning and Celia and Anne and I all said good night to the Smits and went back on board *Transcur*. "I'll help you clear up the mess" I said, "and then you and Anne can sleep until the boys wake you in the morning. I'll get everything ready for beaching and the pump."

The water was now coming in steadily and the pump was going almost continuously. It would run dry every twenty minutes or so and then it had to be switched off for five minutes, by which time the water would have risen again to within six inches of the cabin floor. Every time it was switched on, after its five minutes rest, it would race with a high pitched whirr, and then it would suck water and the note would suddenly drop two octaves. At the same time one could hear the discharge splashing into the calm harbour. I helped Celia and Anne to put the floor boards down in the cabin and then we attacked the mound of

106

gear on Celia's bunk and got it all stowed away somewhere. Anne changed into her nightdress, got straight into her bag and was gently snoring within two minutes. Celia came out into the cockpit for a last good night. "Will you be all right without sleep?" "Yes, I must stay up to watch the pump and to see that she doesn't sink with all of us fast asleep inside her. I've got to get the sheer-legs ready for the morning and there are a hundred jobs to be done." "Do you think she will really be all right?" Celia asked. "I don't know. We'll see when we get her on the beach. She must be as strong as hell to stand that pounding." Celia said "The boys came out of that lot best. Not one single complaint."

As soon as Celia was asleep I turned the cabin light off and drew the curtain across the alleyway. Everything was quiet now except for the low purr of the pump. I sat down opposite the galley and started to fill my pipe, methodically packing the tobacco in and pressing it down. It was nice and warm and comfortable sitting there and my brain was beginning to slow down after the mad race of the last eight hours. Even if the boat turned out to be really badly damaged—maybe a split plank or a timber stove in—at least we were all together again, and no one was harmed. Everyone was asleep in their own beds, as Patrick and Adrian had wanted so much, so things couldn't be so bad. Furthermore we had stalwart friends who as well as being helpful were intelligent and practical and I felt that all of us, together with what resources Terschelling might have to offer, would surely find a way of patching the old girl up. What we were to do next I had no idea—that would be a question to be answered at leisure. Leisure—my half filled pipe slipped to the floor and my head rested comfortably against the side of the coach roof, my msucles went limp and relaxed and a feeling of peace slowly spread through me, starting at my feet and working its way round until I slipped into a kind of trancelike state midway between sleep and wakefulness. I stayed like this for a few minutes and would have fallen fast asleep if I had not been startled into consciousness by the pump sucking air again, and its note changing as if it were shouting out to be switched off. It was half past

107

two in the morning and I had a lot to do before *Transcur* would be ready to be beached.

First of all I went round the deck in the moonlight tidying up the loose gear and putting everything back in its proper place. The anchor was still lying untidily on the side decks with the chain hanging in a bight under the boat and I had to ease it overboard with a trip line round it and haul it up again through the fair lead in the bow. The big headsail was bunched up in an untidy heap on the deck and I had to unhank it from the forestay and the halliard and stuff it back into its bag. I noticed with annoyance that our good boat hook had gone and remembered having allowed it to drop overboard, but apart from that all the gear seemed to be intact. I went to the locker under the cockpit, took out all the spare pieces of wood I had on board and selected two short planks which I sawed into flat feet for the bottoms of the sheer-legs, to prevent the legs from sinking into the mud. Then I made wedges which I nailed onto the legs about six inches from the top so that the ropes that would hold *Transcur* upright from the chain plates on each side, would be prevented from slipping down the legs. I got ready all the gear I would need for making a temporary repair—caulking cotton and a makeshift iron, a sheet of lead and copper nails and tacks, seamflex stopping and a tin of patent rubber sheathing which I had once seen advertised as a guaranteed leak stopper. I upended the dinghy from its place on the foredeck and slid it into the water as quietly as possible so as not to wake Patrick in the fo'c'sle, although I knew that wild horses galloping round the deck would not have woken him this night.

By the time everything was ready for us to go it was quarter to four so I made a cup of tea, went on board the boyer to Willem's bunk, identified him snoring steadily and put my hand on his shoulder. He woke up at once and was immediately fully conscious and in command of himself, like a true sailor. "All right, I'll come now" he said and in three minutes he and Jan and the two boys had come on board and were drinking tea.

We slipped our ropes as quietly as possible, started the engine and glided out into the stream. The sky was slowly coming light

108

and the moon showed fitfully from between high, fast moving clouds. Willem strained his eyes to get a bearing from the inner end of the harbour wall. He had already decided in his mind where to put *Transcur* ashore, on the long bank which formed a kind of continuation of the harbour, inwards from the wall. He took us upstream for a few hundred yards and then turned hard to starboard and headed as if to go straight out to sea. "Speed her up a little", he said. We all waited, tense and expectant as *Transcur* gathered increased way and then she hit the bank, coming quietly to a halt as her keel bit into the bottom. "That is good" Willem said "She is just in the right place. I hope the bottom is not too soft." We sent the two boys off in the dinghy to steady the sheer-legs as we lowered them overboard, settling each one firmly on the bottom, and lashing them down to the chain plates with lengths of strong light line cut specially for the purpose. I had taken it for granted when I sent Willem's cousins off in the dinghy that they were competent seamen and in fact, they handled the boat masterfully. By the time we had the sheer-legs fast in position it was already light and the tide was beginning to leave us. I could see patches of the bank drying out to starboard of us; we all sat in the cockpit and talked quietly and drank more tea and waited for the tide to go down far enough for us to be able to walk round the boat.

Willem and Mr. Smit were both ship's engineers. They were both on leave at this moment and were taking their holiday on the "Yalack", which is the local name for what we know as a boyer. The yalack was called *Het Wakend Oog* which means "The Watchful Eye". She was an old boat, probably older than *Transcur*, and Mr. Smit said that she was one of the first to have been built of iron. She had the traditional Dutch rig, mainsail with curved gaff and one big headsail, and she had a diesel engine which Willem and his father had installed themselves—they had bought it second-hand and had converted it from some other use.

The whole family, that is, Willem, Jan, Willem's young sister and the two boys who were cousins, always spent their holidays in the yalack and they usually came to Terschelling because Mr.

Smit is a Frieslander and Terschelling is where he was born and brought up. They themselves now lived much further south, in Utrecht, but several of Mr. Smit's relations were still in Terschelling. Mrs. Smit and her sister always came with them on these holidays to cook and look after the family. Willem was third engineer of a Dutch cargo boat and Mr. Smit was chief engineer of a tanker running from Holland to Curacao and South America. Willem and Mr. and Mrs. Smit all spoke excellent English which was not surprising since English is a favoured second language, particularly amongst sea-going folk. But Willem spoke, in addition, French, Spanish and Russian with varying degrees of accomplishment as well as the sonorous and elegant Friesian language which is now dying out and is only spoken by a few islanders. His age, I supposed, was about 22 or 23. Willem was obviously a great conversationalist—he was always meeting new people and he spent hours talking to fishermen and long-shoremen from whom he amassed a great fund of knowledge about the sea and ships. He had been on the quay engaged in a conversation, when I had brought *Transcur* into the harbour and with his quick intelligence he had at once sized up the situation and had come to lend a hand when he heard the reception I was given by the German motorboat man.

It would have been hard to have found more acceptable helpers than Willem and his charming family. They had deluged us with friendly hospitality and that most valuable of all assistance that springs from sympathy and real knowledge combined. As Mr. Smit had said, this was something of an adventure for them and they threw themselves into it with all their youthful enthusiasm.

As soon as the water went down, Willem and I climbed overboard and walked round the boat. The ground was soft mud to a depth of about nine inches and then sand. *Transcur* was sitting up straight on her keel with the turn of her bilge, where we knew the major leak was, just clear of the mud. She appeared to be not too badly damaged. The major leak was obviously in the planking on the starboard side where the filling and caulking had all been shaken out from between two planks. You could

110

put your finger right up between these two planks and if you bent down with your head just clear of the mud you could clearly see where the caulking was damaged. To my great relief, neither the stern post nor the rudder appeared to be broken, although the caulking had also been shaken out where the planking meets the stern post. I thought it would be possible to make some sort of temporary repair but it was going to be an unpleasant job because the turn of the bilge was close to the mud and one would have to lie in the mud on one's back to be able to see the damaged part. The paint over most of her bottom had been lacerated by the sand and over large areas it was rubbed right off as if some industrious person had spent hour upon hour sanding her down to the bare wood.

As soon as the water had all gone, leaving the slimy mud with its sprinkling of sharp shells and stones, we decided to start. We made a platform on the mud with one of the dinghy floor boards and put on it all the gear I had got ready. Then I took off my clothes and lay down on my back, with the other dinghy floor board under me, directly beneath the leak. It was cold and the mud squeezed up between the gaps in the floor boards and slowly clutched at me with a clammy grip but, provided I had someone to pass me what I needed, it was possible to work. The seam was damaged over a length of about three feet. I raked it out with a scraper and a knife and got it as clean as possible and then I began to hammer in the caulking cotton, up into the seam, getting it as tight as I could. Finally, I filled over the caulking cotton with red lead putty and for good measure I gave the whole area a coat of the patent rubber sheathing.

After an hour of lying flat on my back and hammering up over my head I was exhausted and when I climbed out from underneath I was completely covered with clinging black mud. Celia, having woken from a deep sleep, came out into the cockpit in time to see my naked form like Othello's ghost. Everybody laughed, Willem himself shaking with mirth. We caulked the stern post as best we could and we went carefully round the hull, pushing caulking cotton into any seams which appeared to

111

be damaged. Then I went for a swim in the harbour to clean myself. Anne woke up and she and Celia made breakfast for everybody—scrambled egg and brown bread and butter. In due course Patrick and Adrian emerged from their bunks none the worse for their adventure of the previous night.

"Is Transcur all right now?" Adrian asked matter-of-factly. "We hope so, we shall see when the tide comes up." Later in the morning the tide did come up and *Transcur* floated off the mud. We unshipped the sheer-legs and took her back to her berth alongside *Het Wakend Oog*. Patrick puzzled out the yalack's name, written on a board across her stern, and said to Celia, "Mummy, is she really called Hot Weekend Egg?"

The leaking was much better after our temporary repair and the pump only had to be used once an hour for ten minutes. Willem and I, pleased with ourselves, went ashore to find the owner of the tiny boat yard. We learned from him that his slip was in fact the only one in Terschelling but that the winch was broken down and all the hauling out wires had been dismantled for a refit, making the slip unusable. However, he said, we were welcome to put *Transcur* on legs on the sand beside the slip and his carpenter would work on her in the afternoon and on Saturday morning and do as much to her as he could.

On our way back to *Transcur* I asked Willem why it was that we had not put *Transcur* on the sandy beach straight away, instead of on the muddy and inconvenient bank. "Because the beach belongs to the boat yard and we had not asked permission" Willem replied with typical Dutch attitude towards authority.

For an hour or so we had leisure to relax; when we had cleaned most of the mud off the boat we went ashore for a walk in the town. At the far end of the quay we found an English yacht whom we had known in Brittany four years previously. After lunch we prepared to put *Transcur* ashore again on the sandy beach. Willem and I got everything ready and we ran her out of the little harbour, round to port and straight up by the side of the slip until her keel grated into the sand. We fixed the sheer-legs in position once again, although this time it was not as easy as it had been on the muddy bank. There, the bottoms of the sheer-legs sank an inch or two into the mud and this had kept them steady while they were being made fast and the ropes tightened. But on the sand there was nothing to hold the bottoms of the legs in position and every time someone moved from one side of the boat to the other and rocked her slightly, one of the sheer-legs would float up to the surface. As the legs had been hurriedly improvised it was not as easy to fit them and get them tight as with properly constructed legs.

As soon as the tide went down enough for us to wade in the water we resumed our caulking, aided this time by the carpenter. We were all absorbed in our work on the starboard side, up to our knees in water, when the port sheer-leg slipped and *Transcur* suddenly fell over on her port side. By good luck there was enough water left to cushion her fall and she came to rest quietly without doing herself any further damage and remained lying right over on her port side. The boys were both ashore when this happened, playing on the sand, but Celia and Anne emerged from the cabin startled and indignant. "What on earth has happened?" Celia asked rather unnecessarily, "As if we hadn't had enough alarms in the last couple of days." With *Transcur* heeled over at an angle of forty degrees life suddenly became almost insupportable inside, but it was a blessing in disguise to Willem and me because we were able to get at the bottom on the starboard side more easily and make a much better job of the caulking than we otherwise would have. We worked without a stop for as long as the daylight lasted, caulking as many bad places as we could see on the starboard side and then giving her a coat of the anti-fouling paint which I had on board. Celia and Anne and the boys spent the afternoon ashore and then the boys went to bed early to make up for their lack of sleep the night before.

Trying to live in the boat when she was heeled at an angle of forty degrees was a a strain on everyone's nerves and tempers, but by good fortune both the boys' bunks are on the port side and by shifting their mattresses so that they lay half in their bunks and half up the bulkheads, Celia was able to make them comfortable and they went to sleep like logs when bedtime came. "We'll have to wake up when the tide comes up in the night"

113

I said "and get her back on the legs so that we can do the other side tomorrow. We can't spend another day at this angle."

Late in the evening we all finished work and Willem and his cousins went off to bed. Celia and I walked ashore to have a meal, leaving Anne to make herself as comfortable as she could. It is no easy task to make yourself comfortable in a boat that is heeling over at forty degrees and it was made more difficult for Anne because her bunk is on the starboard side and the angle of heel would tend to throw her out of it onto the cabin floor. All the same she thought she would be able to keep herself in it and to make herself comfortable. "I shall wash" she said firmly before we went "It'll be a good exercise in ingenuity and patience." Celia and I wandered slowly into the town looking for a café and marvelling at Anne's capacity for hygiene even in dire adversity.

We sat down to our meal but we were both too tired to do more than exchange monosyllables. The tiredness had worked its way right into my mind as well as my body so that all thought and action of any kind was a major effort.

"Celia, there's one thing we must remember. We must set the alarm clock before we go to sleep." We struggled through our meal mechanically, Celia prodding me under the table when my eyes closed and my head drooped forward and as soon as we had finished we paid the bill and set off back to *Transcur*. There she was, lying over on her side in the dark, on her little strip of sandy beach. "She looks like an old whore lying there" I thought to myself and for a moment I cursed my subserviance to her and wondered why she should dictate this torment and why I should always feel compelled to follow her strictures. "If I'd had any bloody sense, I'd have left you on the Terschelling bank and claimed the insurance money" I mumbled as Celia and I climbed on board. With a last effort of will I set the alarm clock for three a.m. "Four hours sleep, this is luxury." Then I took my shoes off and placed them carefully on the cabin floor near the head of Celia's bunk just abaft the mast. "I'll know where they are when I get up" I made a mental note. I flopped down into Celia's bunk with my back resting against the cabin table which stows along the bulkhead behind it when it is not in use. I was asleep before Celia came and lay down beside me, covering us both with a blanket, the heel of the ship pressing her warm body against mine.

The alarm shrilled out and its strident note cut its way through the padded wall of sleep. Celia was beside me snoring gently and I climbed over her and stood up in the cabin which was now upright. "Got to switch off the alarm. Yes, that's it, switch off the alarm. I know that's what I've got to do—switch off the alarm." I staggered to the alleyway where the clock and the barometer are fixed to the bulkhead beside each other and fumbled to open the face of the clock. Yes, that's it, there's the little button. "Push alarm, it says, so if I pull, this bloody noise will stop." My fingers found their way round the button and I pulled. At once there was blessed silence and peace again. "Thank Christ for that, now I can go back to bed where it's warm."

I got back under the blanket, felt the warmth of Celia's body through her pyjamas, and curled myself tightly round it. It was nice for *Transcur* to be upright again, I thought, nice to be able to go to sleep without being jammed against the ship's side. I was falling off again fast into the mysterious labyrinth of sleep, but something somewhere was worrying me, tearing away at my consciousness and refusing to allow the black curtain to fall. Very slowly at first it began to be borne in on me that I had got up to fix the sheer-legs and not just to switch off the alarm. "That's right, you've got to fix the sheer-legs, otherwise she'll lie down on the sand again and we won't be able to work tomorrow, because the side we want to work on will be on the ground, and then we'll have to lie another day at that fearful angle and the next day is Sunday so the carpenter won't come and do the caulking and we shall have to stay on this beach until Monday."

Suddenly I was awake, jumping out of Celia's bunk, and I had my feet on the cabin floor. I could see at once that *Transcur* was already beginning to go over. That meant that the tide had been up and was now going down again. Where the bloody hell were my shoes? I'd left them just there, ready to get right into.

One of those God damn women had moved them. Blast the bloody women. "I curse the bloody woman who's taken my shoes" I said out loud, "damn and blast the bloody woman who's taken my shoes." I had it in my mind that I had to have a pair of shoes on and so I went to the clothes locker and looked in the bottom of it. There was a pair of shoes there and I tried to get them on but they must have been Celia's God damn shoes and they wouldn't fit. By this time Anne and Celia were both awake, startled by the general noise and confusion and the bad language. "Your shoes are in the companionway" Anne said, "I put them there so you'd be able to find them easily."

I put my shoes on, went up to the shrouds on the port side and dropped the sheer-leg overboard. I tried to do up the lashing but *Transcur* was already listing to port and I could not get the rope tight. Celia was up when I shouted to her, "Quick, come and help me." We both heaved on the lashing as hard as we could but *Transcur* is a heavy old boat and it was more than Celia and I could do to lift her upright from an angle of about ten degrees. "Oh Jesus, we shall be here for two more days. We'll never get her up now." I was in a blind fury as I heaved and struggled with the lashing and for the first time I began to feel a touch of panic eating away at my capacity to think clearly. It seemed to me that it was a matter of absolute importance to get *Transcur* upright on the sheer-legs. If only I hadn't overslept like a tired child it would have been a simple matter to have put the sheer-legs on.

Celia's calm steady voice cut through my addled senses like a sharp, clean knife. "Why don't you get a rope from the mast and pull her up from the shore, while there's still some water left?" she said. Of course, that was the answer. Brilliant. All the great thoughts of this life are of profound simplicity. If we could get a rope from somewhere up the mast, preferably at the top, and pull from the shore, we might still get enough leverage to lift her. "You're right, you clever creature. Get Anne up straight away. Tell her to come right now." Celia went to get Anne and I unshackled the main halliard from the top of the sail and hauled the bare end up the mast. I knew the splice would not go through

116

the sheave at the top of the mast so that it would jam there and give us a long wire from the mast head. With the main halliards downhaul added to this length we would have plenty of scope and it would be quite strong enough to hold her. When I had overhauled the main halliard and thrown the wire with its downhaul over the starboard side into the water I did the same thing with the foresail halliard and threw it over the port side. By the time both mast lines were ready Celia was back and Anne was beside her, shivering in her blue nightdress.

"Christ, that's a bloody unseamanlike garment" I said to Anne. "Come on, hop over into the water and take the end of this rope. Celia, go over the other side with this one. It's the foresail halliard. Pull the slack through until the block gets to the top and won't come any further and then wait till I tell you what to do." I climbed over the starboard side with Anne and we waded out in the waist deep water with the end of the main halliard, right across the width of the little beach. The moon, that I had seen so much of during the past two nights, was out and the harbour water was calm and shining in its light. The water soaked Anne's nightdress causing it to cling to the contours of her body so that she looked like some Greek siren. We waded out until we got to the end of our line and then we turned and faced *Transcur*, me in front and Anne immediately behind me. "Right, now. Dig your heels into the sand and pull." We both laid back on the rope, in the water to our shoulders now, and pulled with all our strength. Slowly and painfully at first *Transcur* began to lift and as she came up the strain on the rope grew less. In a moment she was upright.

"Steady her on your side Celia", I shouted. "Easy now." I left Anne holding the halliard and waded to *Transcur*'s bow from where I could see that she needed to come a little more. The two girls were hanging to their ropes like circus acrobats on a maypole. "Heave about two feet Anne, you slack up Celia. Right. Hold her there." I climbed on board gingerly, walked up the deck and fixed the starboard sheer-leg while Celia held *Transcur* with the foresail halliard, then Anne pulled hard against the leg while I fixed the one on the port side. "We've done it, you wonderful

117

girls. You can both come back on board. Leave the ropes there, we'll get them in the morning."

A moment later they both hauled themselves up over the bow, standing on the bob-stay to give themselves a purchase while I grabbed their arms and pulled them on board, two dripping sodden creatures that I wouldn't have changed for any crew in the world.

At seven in the morning Willem and his gang came along ready and anxious for more work, on the port side this time. The carpenter had been given another job on a coaster that had just come in and was unable to help us but he gave us some more caulking cotton and some advice, relayed through Willem. We examined the hull again on the port side and found several places where the caulking had been shaken out, but still nothing seemed to be badly smashed as far as we could see. The stern post was the worst part of her, as on the other side, and Willem and I worked all the morning making good as best we could. Jan and the cousins painted the port side as they had done the other on the previous day. Celia and Anne and the boys got up and had their breakfast and then the boys went ashore to play happily on the beach while Celia made another saucepanful of scrambled egg. At lunch time we were finished and in any case, the water was coming up and we could do no more. Soon she floated again and we took her back alongside *Het Wakend Oog*. "We've done all we can do ourselves, without slipping her. We'll just have to see how she is."

Chapter Eleven

After she had been afloat for an hour we could see that *Transcur* was no longer leaking dangerously, although a fair amount of water was still coming in—a quick calculation showed that she would at least last through the night without having to be pumped. We were all slightly disappointed that we had not succeeded in making her completely tight again although this would have been too much to expect after the pounding she had received.

"You are lucky you still have a boat" Mr. Smit said, "Ships that go on the Terschelling bank do not often come off again." Celia and I showed him on the chart the exact spot where we had gone aground. "But the Noordgat is not there now", he said, "There's the channel you should have taken" and he pointed to the Thomas Smit gat. "I can see that now. But how is it the Noordgat isn't there? It's marked clearly on the chart." "Well you see, there was a northerly gale some weeks ago and the Noordgat was closed in by the sand. That is a dangerous place round there. The sand banks move about with the wind." "But what about that?" Celia said pointing to the wording on the chart 'Closed to Navigation'. Mr. Smit shrugged his shoulders. "All this part was heavily mined during the war. They think maybe there might be a few mines left so they put a warning on the chart. Then if you hit a mine it's your own fault—not theirs." "But if the channel is closed to navigation", Celia persisted, "and if the Noordgat is no longer there, why is the channel buoyed at all, at least as far as here?" And she pointed to the spot on the chart where the two channels meet. "The Thomas Smit gat is buoyed right out to the edge of the bank—right out to deep water" Mr. Smit said, "but you did not see the buoys because they are far apart out there and there was too much mist." But he had to agree that it was illogical and dangerous to have "Closed to navigation" written across a buoyed channel and none of us could think of a rational explanation for it.

We decided to take *Transcur* out on a trial sail the next day, which was Sunday, and Mr. Smit and Willem said they would like to come with us. "Then we'll see how much she leaks" Celia said, "and if she's not too bad we'll go on to Denmark on Monday." I looked at Celia in astonishment. Go on to Denmark. I had quite decided in my mind that our Denmark trip was off, that Celia would never agree to continue the cruise after what had happened and that it was just a question of patching *Transcur* up in order to get her home. "After all, we've only been going for a week" she continued, "We've still got plenty of time to go to Denmark." I was elated. I would never have had the nerve to propose that the cruise should be continued if she had not made the suggestion herself. "All right, we'll see how she goes tomorrow." The sky already looked grey and menacing to windward, the glass was falling fast and there were all the signs of a gale coming up so I thought the next day would probably give *Transcur* a fair test.

Now that the work was done we could relax for the first time.

Adrian was provided with a small seat on the back of Willem's bicycle and four of them set off in high spirits to visit one of the Smit's aunts who lived at the far end of the island. We took Patrick for a walk in the village and out on to the sand dunes beyond so that he could show me the full bleakness of the landscape they had walked over. From a little hill outside the village the sand stretched far away to the horizon with not a sign of a

120

house or a farm. It was easy to feel the loneliness of it even in the daytime and to imagine the horror of being lost in it with two small children on a dark night. Patrick pointed vaguely to a hill in the distance. "That's where we had the brandy Daddy" he said. We walked across the sand for a few hundred yards trying to retrace their steps of the previous night but it was a featureless desert landscape of almost biblical proportions. Celia was not sorry to turn away from it and to walk back to the comfortable cabin of *Het Wakend Oog* where Mrs. Smit had invited us to tea.

We were interrupted by a policeman who poked his head into the cabin and asked if the Englishman was on board. I went up and found that the police had brought back our life raft which had been found stranded on the beach way out on the north east coast of the island. The police had loaded it onto their jeep and now they brought it alongside *Transcur* and unloaded it onto the quay. We thanked them cordially and Mr. Smit and I set about expelling the air from the life raft so that it could be stowed aboard. We would not be able to use it again until it had been sent back to the manufacturer to be refolded and packed back in its suitcase, a job we could not do ourselves. We were delighted that such an expensive piece of equipment had been returned to us undamaged. "Your countrymen are very honest" I said to Mr. Smit. Then Willem came back with Adrian, full of gifts from Willem's aunt, happy and ready for his bed. We all revelled in Mrs. Smit's hospitality, Willem got out his accordian and we sang songs and talked on board *Het Wakend Oog* until far into the night.

The next day the promised gale was piping hard from the north-west. Willem and I tucked reefs into *Transcur*'s mainsail, got out the tiny spitfire jib and embarked all the Smit family including the boys and Willem's sister. As soon as we got clear of the harbour *Transcur* put her rail down and stormed out of the entrance channel in the smooth water in the lee of the island the wind whistling through her rigging and the bow wave curling up almost as high as the weather rail. We went out for half an hour until we came clear of the land and *Transcur* began to

121

knock into the short seas and send spray stinging across the deck. Our visitors began to get wet and so we brought her flying up into the wind and sped back to the harbour on the other tack with the gale abaft the beam. Celia was standing just inside the companionway and as we got near the harbour I caught her eye and saw in it an unmistakeable look of bitter disappointment. "What's the matter?" She pointed down along the lee side of the cabin floor and I saw a line of water already creeping up over the boards. In the excitement of the sail I had forgotten about the leaks but there they were again, still with us. Celia shrugged her shoulders and I caught the glint of a tear in her eye as she switched on the electric pump. We came back alongside *Het Wakend Oog* in time for lunch and Willem asked, "Well, how was she?" "Not good enough. She made water up to the floor in that short time. We'll have to get her on a slip somewhere."

The problem was to know where an available slip could be found and a yard that would do the repair. Although I could not be sure, I had a strong hunch that it was the garboard that was leaking—the very bottom of the boat where the planking joins the keel. The garboard had been so close to the sand when we had beached her that it had been impossible to caulk it and I figured that if the caulking had been shaken out of the turn of the bilge, the garboard would have been damaged as well—perhaps one or more of the keel bolts had been broken. I knew as well that the stern post needed more attention than we had been able to give it. It had been badly strained and in fact it had moved its position—we could tell that this was so because the tiller would no longer travel past one of the boom crutch stanchions whereas before there had been over an inch of clearance for it. The stern post must have moved and, of course, the rudder with it to close this gap.

Willem and Mr. Smit and I discussed this at length but neither of them knew of a yard that would be suitable. Then an acquaintance of Mr. Smit's who, like everyone in Terschelling, knew about our troubles, came on board to commiserate and to find out the latest news, which by now was a favourite topic of conversation in the village. How the Englander had tried to go through the Noordgat was a subject for talk and head-shaking and conjecture.

This friend of Mr. Smit's, whose name by coincidence was also Smit, evidently had powerful friends in high places and he took me ashore to see the director of a salvage company which had tugs and ships in Terschelling. Smit and I told the Director the whole story. There was much nodding of the head and a long conversation which I didn't understand and finally we went to see another very old and apparently immensely important man, who lived in a big house near the quay. Peter Smit and I were ushered into his presence.

He sat in his big armchair in a beautiful room full of priceless porcelain, china, and sombre Dutch paintings. He scrutinised me with a sharp bright eye as Peter repeated the story. Then there was a long silent pause. I was uncertain what to do or say as the silence spread into minutes; the bright eye seemed to bore into me, piercing each protective sub-conscious layer until everything in me was laid bare—open for him to read at will. Desperately I said to Peter "Tell him my wife wants very badly to visit Denmark." Peter translated and the ghost of a smile flickered over the heavy features. He picked up a telephone from the table beside him and spoke into it for five minutes. Then he uttered a few quick sentences to Peter and in a moment we were outside in the street. I felt the sweat running down inside my shirt. Then Peter said to me "You are to have your boat at the Welmerlegen shipyard, in Harlingen, at eleven o'clock tomorrow morning. When you get there you are to ask for Mr. Ogerfoorst."

The next day was Patrick's birthday. We were all up early, Patrick unwrapping his presents and bubbling with excitement. The Smit family all came on board. Willem had his accordian with him and everyone sang "Happy Birthday To You" in Dutch and then in English. Each of the Smits shook Patrick by the hand in turn and solemnly gave him their compliments on reaching the age of eight. The pride and pleasure shone out of his face; this little ceremony exactly suited Patrick's nature. It gave him pleasure, as it would to any small boy, to know that his birthday was considered an important enough occasion for even Mr. Smit and Mrs. Smit to come specially on board to shake him by the hand.

It had been agreed that Willem should come with us to Harlingen, from where he proposed to travel to his home to make some arrangements about his next trip to sea. With much handshaking and fond good-byes we let go our ropes. We had presented Mr. Smit with a bottle of English gin, which he greatly prized, and Willem with a copy of *Cruising Under Sail* which we had with us. We cleared the harbour with Willem at the helm and as we drew away the Smit family, as well as many other well-wishers, came and waved to us from the quay. Celia and I had lumps in our throats. Anne said to Willem "It will be a long time before we meet another family so kind and good as your family." Indeed they were splendid people, taking their pleasures simply and together, enjoying life to the full and never happier than when they were helping someone in trouble. Celia and I reflected that the world could not be such a bad place when such people are still to be found. We all waved from the deck and blew a salute on our fog horn.

The gale had melted away to a gentle northerly breeze and we set our big headsail and ran with the wind up the channel we had come down only four days previously. When we got to the Pannengat we turned off to port and headed towards Harlingen. With the wind light and fair and the sea smooth *Transcur* did not leak overmuch but we still pumped for a few minutes every half an hour.

Willem told us that the Welmerlegen was a big repairing yard which handled ships up to 20,000 tons and we were not quite sure what to expect from it. Willem had never heard of a yacht being slipped there before.

We soon picked out Harlingen standing clear of the low countryside with its towers and tall shipyard cranes. We were late—it was after twelve when we passed through the swing bridge and saw the yard in front of us. It was an awe inspiring sight from the deck of a yacht. Great cranes towered into the air above half a dozen ships ranging in size from a 2,000 ton freighter to a huge tanker. The ships were laid beside one another in neat rows and all of them were alive with men on ladders and stages, with paint brushes, chipping hammers, arc welding torches giving off a blue Martian light and cutting torches sending down streamers of golden rain. There was a noise which one associates only with shipyards; hammer on iron, the whine of electric motors, the staccato of rivetting machines and the occasional clash of iron plates as they were lowered to the ground by one or other of the cranes.

As we glided alongside in the still, oily water we heard above the general din a girl's cool voice through the loud speaker system. Willem translated for us. "Mr. Ogerfoorst to the telephone please" or "Will Mr. Ogerfoorst please go to dock No. 5" or "Mr. Ogerfoorst is wanted in the Director's office." We were all struck silent by this unbelievable place. What possible niche could *Transcur* find for herself here? Then Celia said incredulously "Isn't Mr. Ogerfoorst the man we are supposed to ask for?"

I looked at Peter Smit's instructions which I had scribbled on a piece of paper. "Yes, my God. It is." It was quite clear that Mr. Ogerfoorst was the hinge pin of this vast enterprise and we wondered how he would take to our small problems. A barge was lying at the foot of the slipway and as we breasted gently alongside it the whistle blew for the lunch break and we saw hundreds of men climbing down ladders from stages high up on the iron cliff of a tanker's side, emerging from under the bulbous bottom of a big freighter and all streaming out into the town from the main gates in search of their lunch. The din was suddenly turned off and it was still and quiet among the monoliths.

An hour later the men climbed back to their perches, the whistle shrilled and the volume was turned up once more. The boys and I went ashore, leaving Celia and Anne and Willem to square up on board. I walked up through the yard, two silent and round eyed boys clutching my hands, under the huge screws and rudder of a tanker, beneath the bottom of another and round the flared bows of an ocean freighter. We came to the administrative offices and went into a small sparse reception room where a girl sat behind a desk.

"May I see Mr. Ogerfoorst please?" "Your name sir?" she said in English. "Mulville." "Ah yes, from the ship Transcur?" She flipped through an index and withdrew a white card. "Just one moment sir." She went through a glass panel, picked up a microphone and we heard the voice "Mr. Ogerfoorst to the office please." Then she said to me "Will you please wait one moment sir?" We sat down in a row on a leather bench against the wall, all of us feeling small and slightly frightened. "Will Transcur really be hauled out on that slip?" Patrick asked. "Perhaps they'll lift her with a crane" Adrian said. After five minutes the telephone shrilled and then the girl said "Would you please go back to your ship. Mr. Ogerfoorst will be there in half an hour." We walked back through the yard, past machine shops where ships' plates were being cut to size, a foundry and an engine shop. The yard was neat and clean and tidy and it seemed that every nut and bolt must be in its proper place. We threaded our way back to *Transcur* round and under the ships. Adrian wanted to see the big crane so we paused and watched while it deftly picked up a bundle of iron plates from the other side of the yard, whisked them way up in the air and lowered them on the bridge of a tanker—one remote man controlling its graceful movement from a glass cabin high in the blue sky.

Back on board I said to Celia "Mr. Ogerfoorst is coming to see us in half an hour." *Transcur* looked incongrous and slightly pathetic in this wilderness of iron and steel and modern efficiency. "I didn't see a single wooden boat, or even a piece of wood if it comes to that, I hope they don't think Transcur is an iron gin-palace."

In half an hour to the minute Mr. Ogerfoorst came briskly down the slip, jumped on to the barge and shook hands. He was tall, young looking, and fair—dressed in a spotless white boiler suit. He had pale blue penetrating eyes which darted round taking notes and appraising every small detail; if they sent back to his brain any messages not to the immediate point they gave no sign of it. He spoke English adequately and he interspersed his remarks with the word "Impossible" barked out between sentences as if it were a form of punctuation. He began to shoot questions. "Is the keel of your ship straight or curved? What is

126

the distance between the stern post and the bow? Impossible! Is the keel of wood or of iron? Do you know where she is leaking? Impossible! Has the ship got ballast inside? What is the weight of your ship? Impossible!" We could see that the tankers and freighters in the yard were all hauled out and launched sideways on a series of enormous iron chocks which moved up and down on rails and were held in position by chains which looked like vast bicycle chains. *Transcur* would have to sit between two of the chocks and the difficulty was that there was no way of supporting her in the centre of her keel, in the space between the chocks. They were spaced in such a way that the forward one would come just underneath the turn of her bow and the after one at the stern post.

Mr. Ogerfoorst walked round *Transcur* taking in every detail of her construction. "We will do it if you wish" he said, "Impossible. But if she breaks in the middle" and here he put his two fists together and bent them downwards making a cracking noise in the back of his throat, "it is your responsibility not mine." I thought for a moment. "I'll take out the inside ballast so that she will be lighter in the centre section. All right, I'll take the responsibility." "Impossible. We will haul you out at half past four this afternoon."

Mr. Ogerfoorst made one more remark before he left us which indicated that he had his reservations about us and about the prospect of repairing *Transcur* in his yard. "You know, this is going to cost a lot of money", he said "a lot of money." I didn't blame him for his apprehension. It was incredible to me that they had even agreed to take *Transcur* on the slip in this great yard, and I knew that it was only through the influence of the all powerful old man in Terschelling that it had been achieved. Apart from *Transcur* being a quite unsuitable boat to be repaired in such a yard, we ourselves cannot have inspired very much financial confidence. We were all more or less dirty, having had our domestic lives turned upside down for the past four days and our normally clean and neat boat was suffering in appearance as well as in her timbers from the knocks and bangs she had been subjected to. In addition, she was obviously very old and no

127

one could be expected to have a very old boat if they were not also poor. Mr. Ogerfoorst may justifiably have suspected us of being one of that ramshackle fraternity of boaters who somehow manage to drag themselves from port to port on a shoe-string and who can be seen now and again in most harbours. To add the finishing touch, I had not shaved for a week and my face was in the nebulous state between beard growing and laziness which doesn't help in financial transactions. The image we projected was not that of a prosperous English family on a yachting holiday. "Yes, I understand that it will cost a lot of money" I said and Mr. Ogerfoorst strode away to make his dispositions muttering "Impossible, impossible" under his breath.

Celia and Anne took the boys ashore. "Keep them ashore until tea time. By then we'll have the ballast out and she'll be on the slip." Once we had the boat to ourselves, Willem and I lifted the cabin floor boards and set to work taking up the heavy bricks of lead. It was a warm afternoon and we began to sweat so that our clothes were soon soaked and streams of perspiration ran down our faces. One of us worked in the bilge, swinging the pigs to the other in the alleyway, who placed them on the cockpit floor. After ten minutes the pile in the cockpit would be moved onto the barge and then we would reverse positions and continue as before. It took us nearly three hours to prise up the pigs, which had been carefully laid in the bilge close together like paving stones, and transfer them all to the barge. In all, we shifted nearly two tons of lead from the centre of the bilge and when we had finished, *Transcur* floated high above her normal marks, seeming to sit on the water like a toy balloon.

Willem and I washed ourselves, put the floor back and tidied the cabin. "I must go now" he said, "to get a train to my home", and we shook hands for the last time. I stood in the cockpit and watched him walk through the yard, giving him a final wave as he paused and looked back from the gates. I wondered how I would have fared if Willem had not come along at the precise moment he was most wanted, and, if it came to that, how I was going to manage now that he was gone. He was a rare bird, Willem was, the like of which one would be lucky to meet again in a hurry. Very few are the men I know whose temperament and outlook on life fit in with my own so closely. Even the dismal experience we had had in *Transcur* had almost been made worthwhile by the making of such a friend.

As soon as Willem had gone I heard the hum of a powerful motor and two of the great chocks advanced down the slip. At the same time the crane came swinging down with two iron posts, fabricated from angle bar of enormous size, which were lowered to the waiting hands who bolted them onto the outside of the chocks, making a simple cradle. Then the motor hummed again and the chocks were lowered down over the edge of the slip and submerged in the water until only the tops of the cradle were visible. I threw a line ashore to one of the hands who pulled *Transcur* along the cill of the slip until she was positioned correctly in the cradle. I agreed by sign language with the foreman that the bottom of the stern post should come down in the centre of the after chock and when she was in position I lashed her to the cradle so that she could not move forward or aft. Then the machinery hummed again and very slowly the chocks began to lift and slide up the slip with *Transcur* firmly astride them. Slowly she lifted and as soon as she began to come clear of the water we could see that she was correctly placed. She was hauled smoothly up until she was about thirty feet from the water's edge and there she came to rest. A solid trestle was placed under the keel between the chocks and wedges hammered in until she was supported in the centre of the keel as well as at both ends. Mr. Ogerfoorst came to see that all was well and seemed relieved that *Transcur* had not broken her back. "You have a strong ship" he said "Impossible. We will start work at half past seven in the morning."

Anne and Celia and the boys came down through the yard picking their way between the ships, having exhausted the possibilities of Harlingen in one afternoon, and we all walked round *Transcur* to see if we could see any more damage. She was in a perfect position to be worked on—far better than on any boatyard slip. She sat high above the ground and you could almost walk upright under her keel. As Willem and I had thought, the caulking was shaken out along part of the length of the garboard but apart from that and the fact that we knew the stern post had been strained, there was nothing bad to be seen. The iron keel band had been broken by the pounding on the sand and part of it was hanging loose but it did not seem likely that she could leak through this band. We were able to examine the ends of the keel bolts but they appeared to be sound. She sat up twelve feet above the concrete floor of the slip and the boys had to climb up a long ladder to get on board.

It was strange to stand on deck surrounded by ships and cranes and the hubbub of the yard. "What a funny place to be on my birthday," Patrick said, and then he thought for a moment, "What about my birthday cake?" We all suddenly remembered that it was his birthday. We went inside the cabin, Anne made tea and Celia found his cake in a tin hidden at the bottom of the food locker where it had been stowed when we left home. Celia made us all go outside while she placed it on the cabin table and lit Patrick's eight candles—then we came in and saw the splendour of it, a big round white cake with a Viking ship boldly drawn in brown and red icing. The candles sparkled in the dim cabin, their flickering light reflecting in Patrick's round shining eyes as he looked at it in wonder. "Oh what a cake" he said "What a fine Viking ship. We'll be able to see a real Viking ship when we get to Denmark."

Chapter Twelve

Mr. Ogerfoorst's remarks about the cost of hauling *Transcur* out in his yard made a deep impression on me and I began to wonder how much the job was really going to cost. Having work done in shipyards, I felt sure, was no poor man's game and when I looked round at the complicated machinery, the droves of highly efficient workmen and the great ships from all over the world that were there, the whole thing began to look remarkably expensive. However, I reflected, *Transcur* was insured and I could see no reason why the insurance company should not pay for the work. Before we had left Terschelling I had thought it best to let the company know what was about to take place at their expense. I had found out that there was no Lloyd's agent in Harlingen and so we had sent a cable to the company in London. "Yacht Transcur damaged on Terschelling bank. Arranging repair Welmerlegen Yard Harlingen. Please ask your Harlingen agent to contact us at yard on arrival." No agent had been to see us so I thought all I could do was to arrange for the repair as best I could and hope they would agree to pay for it. I felt a tinge of guilt about the insurance company because I knew that our annual premiums, faithfully paid ever since we first had *Santa Lucia*, would by now just have covered the cost of our last major claim when *Santa Lucia* had been crushed in

131

the Parksluis in Rotterdam. I felt it was hard that the insurance company should not have even a brief term with our profit and loss account in the black before it plunged down again. Of all the expenses connected with boating Celia and I find the insurance premium is the easiest to bear cheerfully and we have never grudged the company their annual cheque. We know that they pay claims promptly, generously and without argument. The premium is a small price to pay for the comfortable feeling inside that even if the worst happened and we lost *Transcur* we would still have a capital sum to go towards buying another boat.

Celia and I always tell ourselves that boating is not an expensive pastime and this is true so long as one makes a proper distinction between capital and running expenses. Maintenance expenses on a boat, even an old one like *Transcur*, are not high provided you are willing and able to do the chores like painting and scraping and varnishing yourself. We pay a very modest annual fee for our mooring in Bradwell and the bill for laying up in a mud berth for the winter does not run into two figures. Sails and rope and paint account for a few pounds over the year but no more than any recreation could be expected to cost. In return we get the endless joy of the sea and the breeze on every summer weekend and for our holidays, abroad or at home, we pay slightly less than it costs us to live normally.

The capital account is a different matter. We lavish improvements on our boat and her gear to the limit of our resources. Celia did raise a faint protest when we changed the ballast from iron to lead. "Surely you're not going to spend all that money on lead" she murmured, but when the job was done and she found that by lowering the cabin floor she had been enabled to stand up straight when she did the washing up, she was reconciled to it. But we had become so conditioned to boating without any money at all in our first years with *Santa Lucia* that we could not help feeling appalled at the prospect of Mr. Ogerfoorst's bill in Harlingen. I sat down in *Transcur*'s cabin after the boys were asleep and wrote a long letter to the insurance company telling them what had happened in the greatest detail.

132

Sharp at half past seven the next morning three men came down the slip armed with caulking irons, mallets and rolls of tarred hemp and began work without delay. They raked out the garboard seams, dried them with a gas blow lamp and set to work hammering the new caulking into the seam on both sides of the hull. I searched the bottom for weak spots, making big crosses with a piece of chalk wherever I saw a place where the caulking had been shaken.

The men spoke no English but we communicated quite successfully, as can always be done on these occasions, by each talking in our own language; by this method our meanings were often dulled but the main points were none-the-less made clear. To communicate refinements, a common language may be necessary, but the essentials of life can always be quite well understood regardless of language.

I wanted to put a lead tingle round the top of the stern post, where it meets the bottom planking, but as the rudder could not be taken out, this was a very difficult job. The four of us worked all the morning in perfect unison with Mr. Ogerfoorst paying us an occasional visit. "Where did you get the lead?" he snapped at me when he saw what I was doing. "I always carry some on board" I replied. "Impossible. You are well equipped" he said. Celia and Anne took the boys ashore in the morning as we thought it best that the children should be out of the yard as much as possible. The caulking was finished at lunch time and I had to restrain Mr. Ogerfoorst from putting *Transcur* straight back in the water. "I haven't finished making my lead patch yet" I complained "and your stopping is not dry yet." "Very well, we will launch you at half past three. Impossible." he said firmly. To the minute, the electric machinery began to hum and *Transcur* was gently slid into the water again. She was pulled back to her berth alongside the barge and as soon as she was made fast the foreman and I peered into the pump well under the floor boards. As far as we could see, next to no water was coming in. "Is good" he said, "Yes" I agreed, "Is good."

The foreman and two of his men helped me to stow the ballast back in its place and *Transcur* sank to her marks once more.

I put the floor boards back, got out a bottle of gin and the four of us raised our glasses. "Is good" they said, "Yes, is good, cheers."

I walked up through the yard and into the cool glass office where the girl sat behind her desk. She was queen in the centre of her technological hive; she issued her commands through her chromium microphone in the detached voice of supreme power so that even Mr. Ogerfoorst came at the run. She was a proto-type of the ultimate woman who, in the final analysis we shall all meekly obey, whose caress is the iron grip of the ship yard and whose bounty is the weekly pay envelope. Mr. Ogerfoorst appeared in his spotless overalls and we walked together through the yard to another block of offices. "We have done as much as we can do. Is the leak mended?" he asked. "As far as I can see at present it seems to be stopped. At least it's very much better." We came to a small office where half a dozen clerks were busy with their ledgers. Mr. Ogerfoorst spoke to one of them, our white card was taken from an index and the clerk went to a typewriter and began to compile our invoice. "How much is the bill?" I asked. Mr. Ogerfoorst glanced over the clerk's shoulder at the white card. "Sixty pounds". "Sixty pounds?", now it was my turn, "Impossible" I said. I had made my own calculation of what the bill might be, allowing what I thought was a maximum for the men's time and the use of the great slipway and I had reached a figure of about thirty-five pounds. Even allowing for overheads—the use of the yard, Mr. Ogerfoorst, the girl with the microphone, I still did not see how the bill could come to sixty pounds but I knew by ex-perience that any job done to a boat always costs far more than is estimated. "If you say the cost is sixty pounds I will have to accept it", I said, rather sullenly to Mr. Ogerfoorst. "Sixty pounds?" he laughed, "I said sixteen pounds. Do you think we are robbers?" I thought I detected a softer look in the flint eyes as we shook hands and said good-bye. "Thank you for every-thing you have done for us."

Celia and Anne and the boys had returned from the town when I went back on board with the Welmerlegen receipt clutched in my hand.

"Guess how much it cost?" I said to Celia. "Thirty pounds." "You're wrong—sixteen". "Vive Mr. Ogerfoorst." "Is the job all right?" Anne asked, "Is she still leaking?" "Certainly nothing like as much as she was" I replied.

Patrick and Adrian were excited at the prospect of going on— they had had enough of Harlingen. They had wandered round the town with Celia and Anne until they knew every road and every shop and they both wanted to be moving again. "Transcur will be all right now, won't she?" Patrick said, "Can we start today?"

We moved *Transcur* out through the swing bridge and found ourselves a berth alongside the picturesque town quay. Here, the children played on the quay and in the dinghy while Celia and Anne cleaned the cabin and got rid of the mess and muck that inevitably accumulates as soon as a boat goes near a slip. I checked over the gear and made ready for sea. We all listened to the evening weather forecast—we had not bothered about the weather for the past three days—which gave us the encouraging promise of a light north-westerly breeze the next day. We bought a new boat-hook to replace the one we had lost on the Ter-schelling bank, filled the tanks with petrol and water and re-stocked the food lockers. There was a good restaurant near the quay and for the first time the three of us went to have dinner together leaving the boys asleep within hearing distance. We drank Old Geneva while we waited for our dinner and watched the quiet orderly Dutch going about their sober and orderly business up and down the quay.

Celia and Anne were full of hope and expectation for the next part of our trip but, perhaps under the influence of the Old Geneva, or perhaps because I was tired, I was remorseful and gloomy. I felt that so far the trip had been a fiasco from the beginning. I had made one miscalculation after another and brought us to the very edge of disaster and now, although the crew seemed to have survived the ordeals inflicted upon them, the boat was in a poor state and my own morale as low as it had ever been. *Transcur* certainly seemed to be leaking much less after Mr. Ogerfoorst's attentions but we had not yet taken her

135

sailing and I had little doubt that she would make water if pressed hard to windward. Nothing short of a thorough overhaul in a really good boat building yard would restore her to her old strength and seaworthiness.

As for myself, I was suffering from tiredness, too much Old Geneva and a crisis of confidence in my own abilities. "Don't be an ass", Celia said, "didn't you get her off the sand when most people would have screamed for help and abandoned her? Now she's had a good temporary patch up she'll be all right to finish the holiday and then we'll get Mr. Drake or someone to fix her up properly when we get back." "Listen", Anne added, "you've saved the boat and you've saved a big insurance claim. You don't have to worry. You've done fine."

"All right, I know I got her off the sand. But who put her on the sand?" Certainly there's an old adage in the Navy; it doesn't matter if you run a ship ashore, so long as you get her off again and write a good report about it. This seemed to be holding good in my case, because so far, everyone who had heard about our adventures had only been full of praise and admiration for our efforts to save *Transcur* and not a single person had asked what I had been up to in putting her ashore in the first place. All very well, this, but I knew inside myself that if I had been doing what I ought to have been doing—using the lead— she would never have gone aground. This was the inescapable fact that I could not help being depressed by—particularly after a few glasses of Old Geneva. Where I had been brought up, to put a ship on the beach was a crime for which you lost your ticket and your job. The old mate I had been with in tugs during the war would have turned white if he had known what I had done.

"All right", I said, "we'll go out tomorrow and if she still makes water badly we'll go into Terschelling again and then crawl back to Ijmuiden through those bloody canals."

The weather was true to its forecast as we left Harlingen the next day, except that the wind was south-westerly instead of north-westerly as promised. This suited us better because it allowed us to fetch up the Takkengat and when we came back into the main stream we let the sheets free and allowed the gentle breeze and the fair tide to carry us back towards the Terschelling bank. As we passed Terschelling itself once again, nothing was said about not continuing the cruise. She was leaking a bit but not an alarming amount, although in such a light breeze and a calm sea she could not have been expected to leak—if she had done so it would have told us quite clearly that she was unseaworthy. As we came up to Terschelling the wind veered round to the north-west as expected, making it most advantageous for us to go out the same way as before, but this time through the Thomas Smit Gat.

Celia was against this plan. "I'd rather go the long way round even if it is twenty miles further and even if we do have to beat to windward for an hour or so." But I refused to do this, and Anne agreed with me. "I promise I'll turn back" I conceded finally, "if we don't pick up the buoys in the Thomas Smit channel."

We were all tense and on edge as we passed along the familiar coast line of Terschelling Island. Celia was in a state of nerves, Anne was grim and silent and Patrick and Adrian were in the cockpit scanning the shore for familiar landmarks. "Look Mummy" Patrick said "there's the gap in the sea wall where we turned inland", There was no mist now, although visibility was not more than three or four miles, and the featureless sandy shore looked bleak and grim. If we had been able to see it as clearly as this before, we probably would not have acted as we had done. It was a moon-like landscape—craters and desolation. Celia shuddered "If I never see that place again, it'll be too soon" she said. We picked up the buoys quite easily, just as we had done before, until we came to the big buoy at the corner. For a few minutes we could see nothing beyond it. Celia said "Look here, let's turn round and go back. I don't like this one little bit and neither do you." The sand banks were hissing and roaring over on our port side, a noise that filled us all with the greatest uneasiness and the seas on them were playing the same old dancing game, leaping savagely into the air in terrifying confusion. We knew what it was like to be in their grip and

137

it was an embrace we did not wish to experience again. I said, "All right, if we don't see the next buoy when we come up with this one, we'll turn back." I was against turning back partly because it would waste time—we would be dead into the wind's eye until we gained the main channel again—and partly because of a streak of obstinacy in me that wanted to see this conflict out to its logical end. I knew there was a channel out there, not only because of the chart but because I had seen the coaster go out that way, and I was damned if I was going to be scared out of following it by a lot of hissing dancing waves plugging their psychological warfare at me.

In a few minutes Anne, with her sharp eyes, saw the next buoy up to port, seemingly in the centre of the turmoil of the breaking shallow seas. "All right, that's the way we go." I said. We came abreast of the corner buoy and turned hard to port, hauling in the sheets as *Transcur* came round. Although there was by no means a lot of wind it was very rough and she began to throw herself about as soon as we turned and brought the seas on the beam. One of the lockers under the galley stove sprung open as she rolled to starboard and cups, tea pots, spoons and plates flew out across the alleyway and into the quarter berth. When she rolled the other way I saw a box of toys on Anne's bunk take off, so that bears and boats and cars became airborne for a crazy moment. The boys were clinging one to each of the cockpit coamings. Adrian looked at me earnestly and said in a small voice "Daddy, are we going to go on the sand bank again?" I gave Celia the tiller and went up the side deck, clinging to the weather runners for support, and swung the lead out ahead. "It's all right, four fathoms."

I stayed up on the side deck taking soundings and peering out ahead for a sign of smoother water. It did seem a bit calmer over to starboard and I told Celia to bear away half a point; it was logical to expect the channel to sweep round in a shallow curve rather than to turn a right angle at the buoy and this fitted in with the chart. All the same it got shallower before we were through and the soundings went down below three fathoms. The water had the same sandy appearance we had seen in the

138

Noordgat and on each side we could clearly distinguish where the banks lay. We passed close to the buoy and soon saw the next and finally the big light buoy which marks the edge of the bank. It began to get smoother, the seas lost their irregular shapes and the soundings went up to six fathoms. I came back into the cockpit "We're through" I said, "we're out in the North Sea again, thank Christ."

Soon after we passed the light buoy we saw the Terschelling light vessel out on our port bow and we bore away and set course for the Borkum Riff sixty miles on. Then the sun came out and all the tensions went out of us. The sea was calm and blue; two lines of shipping one going east and the other going towards the English Channel stretched as far as the eye could see to both horizons; the boys started a game in the cabin and the boat was full of their laughter. Celia made tea and she and Anne and I sat in the cockpit sipping, relaxed in the silence that comes with relief. *Transcur* settled down to an easy pace in the light air, a line round her tiller to keep her on course. The innocent looking island of Terschelling, reflecting the bright sunshine from a long strip of yellow sand slipped away into the realms of memory out to starboard of us. Celia yawned and then said, stubbornly, "I still think it would have been better to have gone round by the main channel instead of through that horrible passage." "Don't worry" I said to her "you can forget about the Terschelling bank now. It's gone for good. Now we can start enjoying ourselves."

Chapter Thirteen

The time was two fifteen and it was Wednesday afternoon, the weather was fine and sunny, the glass was high and the wind, what little there was of it, had veered to the north so that it was just before the beam of our course of 072 degrees.

Transcur sails very nicely with the wind just before the beam; you can lash the helm and she will steer herself for as long as you like to leave her, slowly luffing until the mainsail begins to lift near the mast and then bearing away half a point until the weight of wind in the mainsail increases enough for her to repeat the process. The ability to steer herself for hours on end without attention is one of *Transcur*'s most useful and endearing accomplishments and one that is very rare indeed—particularly in boats of modern design. Most modern ocean racers and cruisers demand constant attention at the helm. You can't leave it even for a minute to go and attend to some chore below or to the fore deck, without the boat taking a wild dive off course and sheering away to one side or the other—often to leeward. This means that two people at once have to be on watch for comfort and even safety.

The ability to sail herself is by no means the only respect in which the old smack has the edge on boats of modern design; she has another virtue which although a simple one is rare enough in a modern boat. She sails upright. She seldom heels at an angle greater than twenty degrees even in a strong wind. Modern boats, almost without exception, heel over at twenty degrees going to windward in no more than a fresh breeze and when it blows hard they sail on their ears. This makes life below wearing and unpleasant. You can't cook without standing on your head, you can't have a meal in comfort and you can't sleep in the weather bunk without being lashed in. These boats are so light that they are thrown about in a sea-way like boxes of matches and to move inside you have constantly to hold on to the hand grips specially provided for this purpose. Even for adults, life in these circumstances saps the energy and frays the nerves but to go to sea in such a boat with small children would be next to impossible. In *Transcur* we can always have a meal from the cabin table in safety and the children can play inside happily and without discomfort. In the days when *Transcur* was built the world was a saner and more orderly place; there was a quality of solidness about life which is reflected in her design.

We settled down thankfully and happily to our sea routine after the anxiety and confusion of the past week. Our original plan for the Danish cruise would have to be modified. We would go to the Baltic through the Kiel Canal and not by the longer route through Lim Fiord as we had intended. Once there, we would see how much time we had left and decide on the best route back when the time came. It would be a shame to come back the same way as we went, but Celia and I thought that this was probably what we would have to do, except that we would miss out Holland on the return journey.

When evening came the wind eased and became fluky and variable so that we had to start the engine for an hour. Then it swung right round to the south-east and freshened to a moderate breeze. We set the watches and as the boys were put to bed the wind freshened a little more and then seemed to settle down. As the wind increased *Transcur* picked up her speed like a train pulling out of a station and soon the log began to spin merrily round as she settled down to a speed of about six knots. The breeze was off the shore now so that the sea was calm; it was perfect sailing weather. When it got dark the sky became a vast black field sewn with a thousand million golden stars each sending its calm reflection to remind us of eternity.

Once free of the brash sun, colour comes flooding into the sky so that the night is full of gentle transmutations of purple, silver and gold, making a pageant of incredible beauty, the dilating Milky Way at its core. Past, present and future are brought into one and for as long as the magic lasts time itself seems to reverse its role and become servant instead of master. The breeze was strong enough to kick up a little short sea which *Transcur* went banging and bustling through, sometimes throwing up a curtain of spray which would hang for an instant in the glow of the starboard side light like the green web-like veil of some exotic dancer and then come flying across the deck. The white sail swung across the sky in rhythmic arcs, steady and strong and pure in the soft night light and full of silent power driving *Transcur* on her way.

I heard the fo'c'sle door slide open and Patrick came to the companionway in his pyjamas. "How are we getting on Daddy?" "We're getting on fine. There's a lovely breeze and we're doing a good six knots. You're supposed to be asleep." "I know but I woke up and thought I'd like to come for a little visit." "All right, now you're here, put the kettle on and make some tea." We chatted for a few minutes while the kettle boiled and then Patrick made tea using only the galley light so as not to wake Celia and Anne. "Is Transcur really all right now?" he asked anxiously, "or is she still leaking badly?" "She's still making a fair bit of water but not enough to worry about." "Will we have to go on the slip again in Denmark?" "I don't know. We shall see." He came out into the cockpit to look at the sky and I pointed out to him the Milky Way, the Great Bear, the Pleiades and the fiery planet Mars. "The Great Bear doesn't look very much like a bear. Does the Southern Cross look like a cross?" I packed him off to his bed again and tucked him firmly in. "Now, go to sleep and stay there until the morning." It wasn't such a bad life for a small boy, I thought to myself—dangerous sometimes perhaps, but on the whole better than watching television.

Celia woke up and came to drink the last of Patrick's tea as

Transcur ploughed steadily on through the night. She shivered in the cool air as she pulled on her thickest jersey and then we sat together in the cockpit for half an hour. Soon, with her good eyesight, she saw the loom of the Borkum Riff light vessel fine on the starboard bow where it should have been. It seemed that we were at peace at last and *Transcur* was shaking off the ugly experience of the Terschelling bank and settling down to behave as she ought, sailing fast and comfortably towards a new destination; this is the essence of cruising.

Then Celia saw something unusual coming across our bow from the seaward side. "It looks like a sail" she said, "surely it can't be." But it was a sail, and as it drew nearer we made out a large yacht coming rapidly towards us. We saw a big gaff mainsail, foresail and jib set flying on a long bowsprit. She was showing us her green light and then she altered course to pass astern of us and the red light came into view. "Green to green and red to red, perfect safety go ahead" Celia muttered. As the yacht got closer something about her rig and her shape began to look familiar and when she was no more than a hundred yards off we saw clearly who she was. "It's Dyarchy" we both said at once. There is no mistaking *Dyarchy*—the clean strong lines of her black hull with her varnished top strake showing clearly in the pale light—her tall mast, without the topsail on this night, pointing high above her gaff, the lovely sheer giving to her fore part all the strength and power you could wish for in a yacht— she gave, as she always does, that rare impression of sturdy grace. She was using a steering vane, which we had never seen on her before, but a figure in the cockpit waved vigorously as we passed. It was a nostalgic encounter for Celia and me. We had admired *Dyarchy* ever since we first took *Santa Lucia* to Lymington and saw her lying at her mooring in the river. Since then we have often seen her in the Solent and in the Channel Islands and we have endlessly read descriptions of her in books and magazine articles. We have talked about her off and on for years as being the finest yacht we have ever seen and the unlikely experience of meeting her miles from anywhere in the North Sea, in the middle of the night, struck us as a propitious omen.

143

Celia took over the watch, we pumped the bilge and I climbed into my place in the quarter berth and pulled the sleeping bag up round my chin. Before my eyes closed I caught a glimpse of Celia's face as she struck a match to light her cigarette and for a moment was in the centre of a ball of yellow light. The look of strain and worry that I had seen almost continuously since our voyage began had at last gone and she looked relaxed and happy again. She was whistling softly and as I drifted into sleep I began to wonder what the piece was and to fit together the phrases—those gradually ascending strings in a cadence that seemed to defy the possibility of any logical ending, until the sombre horn came to their rescue and brought them back to reality. Then there was a bassoon—or was it a clarinet—taking us away on a new and inspired incentive, rocking and lilting freely within the tight discipline of the composition. Ah yes, it comes to me now, it's the Schubert Octet. Now that Celia's idle whistle was safely identified, like some light house on our course, it allowed me to fall deeply asleep.

How immeasurably finer a composer was Schubert in his chamber music than in those endlessly repetitive symphonies which go thundering on and on and on. Being denied the use of pure noise by the limitations of the small ensemble, he had recourse only to his endless subtlety and his astonishing inventive genius. Once let loose with a full orchestra he becomes a crushing bore; those deliriously beautiful flights of musical fantasy transform themselves into pure noise, which soon palls. He becomes a Germanic tub-thumper, like Beethoven at his worst. About Beethoven, Mozart said with studied irony having heard him improvising on the piano, "Watch that fellow—he will make a noise in the world one day."

Celia and Anne must both have stayed on watch longer than the agreed two hours because when I woke, completely restored and refreshed, the dawn was already beginning to lighten the sky and the Borkum Riff was way out of sight astern. Nothing of importance had occurred in Anne's watch except the passage of a big liner, well clear of us to seaward, and a visit from a little bird which still perched on the cabin top in the lee of the sky-light out of the wind and the occasional spray which swept across the deck. *Transcur* was still making a good six knots as I saw from the log, the sky still looked fine and the glass was steady. The wind had shifted slightly more to the south and I was able to ease the sheets a fraction so that she would steer herself without attention.

Anne went off to sleep, yawning and stretching, to get what rest she could, before the boys woke up demanding breakfast and attention and that everyone else should be awake as well as they. I switched on the pump and listened to its hum for a good six minutes before it sucked air, which meant that *Transcur* was still making very much more water than she ought. Maybe we would have to slip her in Denmark again as Patrick had suggested. There was no difficulty in navigating across this piece of sea because there were frequent buoys as well as the occasional tall towers on the shore which were sometimes visible although over ten miles distant. There was a continuous stream of shipping passing to and fro to seaward of us which told us that we were on course. It was encouraging and made for interest to have ships always in view, particularly as we could not feel full confidence in the state of *Transcur*'s leaks. On the other hand the charm and excitement of making a passage across a real ocean, as we had done on our trip to Spain, were missing.

Soon after the sun was up Patrick came busily out of his fo'c'sle full of enquiry as to our progress, the state of the leaks and the situation generally. It wasn't long before he woke Adrian who came out bursting with energy. I managed to amuse them for an hour and to keep them from waking Celia and Anne. We tried to feed the little bird, which was too tired to be afraid of us and we at last persuaded it to eat a piece of bacon fat with apparent relish. I thought this would be good protein for it, rather than bread which would do it very little good. People persist in giving bread crumbs to birds although it is a poor diet for them. If you feed a bird exclusively on what passes for bread in our society, it would die very quickly. Soon afterwards the bird took off and made towards the land but the fresh breeze was too much for it. We watched it battle bravely towards the distant

145

shore but soon it seemed to give up the struggle and was swept out into the North Sea to its certain destruction—to fly on for as long as it could sustain its weight in the air and then gradually to lose height until it would skim over the waves, striving for a perch that did not exist in the wild open ocean.

Celia got up and made breakfast and at once the boat came alive with noise and activity. Our fine southerly breeze eased as the sun came up and *Transcur* slowed down to four and then three knots. A few ships began to appear out of the German ports, crossing our bows and making off to the north. In the light sunshine of the forenoon we saw the white plumed bow wave of a destroyer, or perhaps a frigate, coming rapidly towards us. As she got nearer we made out a White Ensign at her peak and we hurried to ship our own ensign staff on the taffrail across the stern. We dipped when she came tearing past and we saw them all wave with enthusiasm as she dipped her ensign in return. It gave us all an involuntary and quite illogical sense of pride and pleasure to see a British warship go past. We were not friendless on the wide sea.

The wind held until we came up with the Elbe light vessel and by lunch time, we had brought it abeam. Then the last light air left us, the sails fell limp and *Transcur* lay quite still on a flat green sea. But we had made a good run from Terschelling covering the 125 odd miles in one hour short of a day. "I suppose we'll have to. start the engine" Celia said "there doesn't seem to be much point in hanging about out here waiting for a breeze."

We had arrived at the entrance to the Elbe just as the ebb tide out of the river was beginning to run and we motored up the buoyed channel making slow progress against the strong current. The buoyed channel seemed to go on for ever across the calm sea and it was not until tea time that we came up with the land, a sandy finger stretching far out to sea which terminated in a low island called Sharhurn, twelve miles to seaward of Cuxhaven. In spite of the air of desolation which surrounded the place we decided to drop the anchor and wait here for a breeze or for the tide to turn so that we would be able to make better progress.

"Can we go ashore?" Adrian asked. There seemed no reason

why not, although the place had a faintly sinister air about it, so we launched the dinghy and the boys and I rowed a quarter of a mile to a gently shelving sandy beach which seemed to stretch for ever in every direction. In spite of the bright sunshine the place was eerie with nothing to be seen but an old hut on a sand dune which was all there was of the island. I began to imagine mines, or quicksands or a firing range and any number of strange hazards. After all, this was Germany and we had no right to be there at all having passed no Customs or Immigration and not having had our passports scrutinized and stamped by a bureaucrat. The sand was hard and clean with firm ripples made by the tide and shallow pools and lagoons—perfect for the children who left their clothes in the dinghy and chased each other up and down the sands and in and out of the water. We saw no one but all the same I was relieved to feel *Transcur's* firm familiar deck under my feet when we went back on board.

We came up with Cuxhaven in the evening just as the tide had begun to run in our favour. "I think we'll go right on up to the entrance to the Canal at Brunsbuttel" I said to Celia "it seems a shame to waste a night in this place when we might be getting on. With the tide under us we shall be up there in a few hours." We had not intended to go up the Elbe at night, particularly as we had no large scale chart of Brunsbuttel Koog and would have to rely on our intuitions to lead us into the locks. However there was a lot of shipping up and down the river and it looked from the chart we had to be quite simple and straightforward. "We'll tie up on this side of the locks for to-night and then we shall be able to go into the Canal first thing in the morning." "All right," Celia said "I'll put the boys to bed before things start to get exciting."

As soon as we got past Cuxhaven the channel narrowed so that the hundreds of ships going into the Elbe, which had been spread out where the river was wide, were jammed tight together, making one continuous line going up the river while another just as dense was coming down towards the sea the other way. The ships were almost nose to tail and suddenly we were part of an endless procession of ten-thousand-ton monsters all

147

tearing through the water at up to fifteen knots. We took up a position as close to the bank as we could, but as the river got narrower the ships came closer and closer so that they would bear down upon us, looming up out of the dark like blocks of flats and rushing past no more than a couple of boats' lengths away.

A fast launch came sheering up alongside full of officials with peaked caps. They harangued us in fast German. "English yacht", we shouted, "English yacht" and shone our torch on the Red Ensign at our stern. "Why you go here night time?" came a gutteral shout "What name of yacht?" "Where your green stern light?" The launch, which was half as long again as *Transcur*, came close alongside turning us all crimson in the glow of his port side lights and smothering our decks with spray from his bow wave. The launch seemed to be edging us more and more into the channel and in the path of the approaching steamers so that we seemed to be in serious danger.

"Where your permit to navigate this river at night?" he shouted. Now he was using a loud hailer and the sound boomed across and through us making all rational thought impossible. "Where your immigration papers?" he boomed again "You must go Cuxhaven and pass Customs." It would be impossible to turn back against the tide now and I knew we would have to go on to Brunsbuttel whatever he said. The next steamer was coming up fast and was already bearing down on our stern. My reserves of patience, such as they are, broke down. "Get out of my bloody way for Christ's sake. We'll be run down in a minute." At that moment Anne, angel of cool reason, came up with the big torch wrapped round with Adrian's green trousers and displayed it on the boom crutch facing aft. At that the German seemed to be mollified and he sheered off in his fast launch muttering something unpleasant through the loud hailer and allowed us to alter course out of the way of the steamer which swept past so close that you could have struck a match on her iron plates as she went by. In the dim light we saw a figure peering down on us from the wing of the bridge, high in the air like God and as her stern came abreast of us the great screw threshing the water, smothered us with spray. All the same, I now know although I

148

did not know then, that the German immigration launch had been quite right to try and turn us back to Cuxhaven. A week or two previously there had been a disaster in the Elbe. An English yacht had been run down and children had been drowned in circumstances very close to our own.

As luck would have it, that night in the Elbe was pitch black and although we had the endless procession of steamers to guide us as well as the channel buoys in the river it was difficult to calculate exactly how far up the river we had come. The flood tide under us was very strong and I was anxious not to miss Brunsbuttel and go on up the river. However, we soon saw that no one in their senses could miss the locks at Brunsbuttel. The channel forked and about half the ships that were going up river turned off to port. At the same time we saw the lights of a small town and in the middle of them something resembling ten Piccadilly Circuses at night. There were enormous clusters of lights round the entrance to the Kiel Canal, green and red and white, all flashing and winking and some sweeping beams round the horizon. Such a confusion that it was quite impossible to distinguish any signal that we could reconcile with our pilot book, or find the lights of the small harbour that we knew was there, just outside the lock.

We slowed the engine down and found ourselves outside the lock gates in the middle of dozens of ships which seemed to be proceeding in every direction. There was a great blaring of hooters and whistles and powerful torches and searchlights were switched on us, illuminating the boat with hard blue light and dazzling us so that we could not see or think. Voices from the night hurled invective at us so that it was quite clear that we were somewhere we ought not to be. "We must get out of this" Celia said "or we shall certainly be run down." Just at that moment it seemed that another set of lock gates opened and a new flood of ships came streaming out across our bows. We dodged between them and went as close inshore as we could trying to find the harbour entrance. Then Anne saw a pale green steady light slightly over to the left and completely outshone by the blaze of illumination to the right of it, which looked as though it might be the harbour entrance and we made our way cautiously towards it. While we paused, hesitantly, in the entrance not quite sure whether we should go in or not, a small coaster came up and we were able to follow him up into the basin and tie up. It was a tiny harbour with nothing but a few yachts and small coasters in it—a haven of quiet after the noise and confusion of the shipping outside, jockeying to get into the Kiel Canal. "I'm not sorry the boys were asleep through that," Celia said with relief.

Chapter Fourteen

Once safely inside the little harbour at Brunsbuttel we tied up alongside the coaster and tumbled into our
beds, quite played out by the excitements of the day. It had
never occurred to me that the Elbe is one of the busiest waterways in Europe, serving the modern port of Hamburg as well
as the entrance to the Kiel Canal and a network of inland waterways. Evidently life on the Continent does not proceed at the
leisurely old-fashioned pace of England. I have now learnt first-
hand what I had read often enough—that Germany is by far the
toughest and most go-ahead country in Europe. To get mixed up
in the sinews of the economic miracle, in the middle of the night,
had been a mistake that only an Englishman with his leisurely
arrogance could have made. No German would have thought
for an instant that a yacht could casually sail up the Elbe in
the night without getting sliced in half, or at best badly frightened. In England everyone stops work at night and there is not
a single river that you could not take a yacht up in comparative
calm. People tend to go to sleep, or enjoy themselves, or both,
at night in England. But in Germany life forges on through
twenty-four hours. Not one minute is wasted that could serve to
make this country richer.

At five in the morning we were woken by the skipper of the

coaster who wanted to go to sea again. For some reason he had foreborne to tell me of his intention before we all went to sleep the previous night. The tide was nearly low by now and as soon as I let go *Transcur*'s ropes and went to move her out of the way so that the coaster could get out, she was aground in soft mud. However, the coaster was light, only drawing three feet of water, and he was able to squeeze past us and steam out of the harbour leaving us foolishly stuck in the mud fifteen feet from the quay. I rowed a rope ashore and then went back to bed vainly trying to store up some sleep, but within half an hour the boys were up, deliciously refreshed and full of interest and conversation about the new place we were in. "Row yourselves ashore" I said sleepily to Patrick "and stay there until breakfast time." They went off and there was peace for half an hour until hunger for breakfast brought them back.

After breakfast Anne and I walked into Brunsbuttel with the shopping bags, leaving Celia to breast *Transcur* alongside as soon as the tide came up. The village looked very prosperous and the shops were full of everything that you would expect to find in some modern English suburb, only more expensive. The boys had large tubs of multi-coloured ice cream. We walked through the village to the great sea locks where shipping was being passed through in a continuous stream both from the Elbe into the Canal and the other way. As well as the ships already in the locks we could see a queue of vessels of all sizes outside, waiting their turn to come in—the same queue that we had got ourselves mixed up in on the previous night.

We made our way across the lock to a small office building, surrounded by green lawns that are always to be seen at locks, and found a charming and helpful man, speaking perfect English, in the office of the United Baltic Corporation. He agreed to look after all the permits and paperwork necessary to pass us through the Canal and told us that he would send his agent on board as soon as we entered the locks, to give us our papers and take a list of any duty-free stores we might want, which would be delivered to us at Kiel when we had passed through the Canal. "We'll send our account to you in England" he said, "and you can pay it when you get back." This seemed an ideal arrangement and we hurried back on board to tell Celia about it. "Do you mean to say we can buy duty free drink, and cigarettes, and stores here, and pay when we get back home?" she asked incredulously. "That's what the man said." "Impossible."

We slipped *Transcur*'s ropes and motored out of the little harbour and round to the entrance to the lock. It was all so easy in the daytime that we wondered how we could ever have become confused. A Dutch and a German yacht were waiting for the lock to open and we stayed with them watching for the semaphore arm on the lock head to give us the signal to enter. Soon the black and white arm moved and we circled round and motored into the lock, tying up near the front and under the bows of a small German cargo ship until the gates opened and we went through into the Canal and stopped alongside a small jetty to wait for the first instalment of our stores.

The agent came on board as promised, bringing all our Canal papers and enough petrol to fill our tank. Celia gave him a long list which he promised to telephone through to his colleague at the Kiel end of the Canal. He had only failed us in one respect and that was to organise us a tow through the Canal. "For the little boats, yes" he said "but the skippers don't like your bowsprit." This was a big disappointment. I had been anxious to get a tow so that we would not have to motor the whole fifty-three miles of the Canal. Our engine had been nothing if not noble through all the vicissitudes of the trip—it had never failed to start at the first press of the button. But it was asking a lot of it to expect it to push *Transcur*'s heavy bulk for fifty-three miles through the Canal and possibly for fifty-three miles back again. I could never get the thought out of my head that the engine shares our mental stresses and anxieties. Surely it will feel it deserves a rest after motoring us off the Terschelling bank? Surely it will never consent to run for another 106 miles up and down this Canal? I can't credit that the engine can be insensible when Celia and I are torn with anguish over some dangerous and difficult situation. It must be aware of its own nobility, or sometimes its perversity and be something more than a collection of cunningly

153

contrived pieces of metal. The engine, I feel, has a soul and deserves equal consideration with any of us.

We started motoring down the canal after a very expensive lunch at a restaurant near the jetty, keeping well into the side out of the way of the stream of ships. The banks of the Canal soon became wooded and rural with occasional vistas over the countryside of Schleswigholstein which was a pleasant agricultural land—not unlike parts of Essex. The wind was blowing across the Canal and was for the most part shielded from us by the high banks so that we had to use the engine continuously and could get little help from our sails. Whenever a likely looking coaster overhauled us we would wave a rope's end and ask pathetically for a tow, but we were always refused.

The volume and diversity of the shipping was extraordinary. The boys soon devised a game of guessing the nationality of passing ships and Patrick drew up a complicated scoring sheet. There were tankers and freighters from twenty thousand tons downwards as well as small German, Dutch and Danish coasters. Sometimes we were unable to identify the ensigns even with the aid of the Nautical Almanac—countries like Kathiri, Gabon, Dahomey and Chad defied identification.

Each time a big ship passed us she would drag the water away from the bank with her backwash and *Transcur* would be remorselessly pulled towards the centre of the Canal. The crews would look down on us waving and laughing at the novelty of an English ensign on a yacht. A big Russian cargo ship exchanged the most cheerful greeting with us, her crew of men and women lining the deck above our heads and waving in a friendly fashion. There were ships of every possible nationality—all the Scandinavian countries, the new African states and a fair smattering of South Americans and even Chinese—but we looked in vain for an English ensign. There were no English yachts either; mostly they were Germans with a few Dutch, an occasional Dane and one French yacht going out towards home again.

We had planned to spend the night at Rensborg, which is just over halfway through the Canal. We had been told that there was a yacht club there and a small harbour. But it was dark by the time we got to Rensborg and in the confusion of lights and ships and ferries we must have passed the club without seeing it. We came to a high-level bridge with a miniature train, all lights like a long glowing insect, passing over it. Anne said, "We ought to get in and tie up somewhere, we don't want another performance like last night". In fact it was essential to find somewhere to tie up because it was strictly forbidden for a yacht to navigate the Canal at night. At intervals along the Canal there were posts and "lay-bys" for ships to tie up in but we could not use these because the wash of passing ships would have made it unpleasant and dangerous to tie up to posts. When we were almost through Rensborg we saw a gap in the bank and we felt our way slowly into a large calm basin with coasters and barges tied up round the edge. We saw a likely place alongside two lightships which were obviously there for a re-fit and we sidled up to them and put our ropes out. We had no sooner stopped the engine when a very fat German appeared and told us in no uncertain way to go, and so we went across to the other side of the basin and tied up to a long steel barge. A man appeared with a small barking dog but just as he was about to tell us to go, it began to rain very hard and the man and his dog disappeared. "I'm not going any further", I said "here's where we stay for to-night."

We tied *Transcur* up, went into our warm dry cabin and turned into our bunks, falling into an overtired, unsettled sleep so that Anne and I both dreamed horrible nightmares. Anne tumbled out of her bed in the night to fend *Transcur* off a train which she heard rattling across the high-level bridge, and which she was convinced was grinding against *Transcur*'s hull, the carriage doors tearing at the bulwarks and wrenching them away from the stanchions.

I dreamed about the lifeboat again. We had drifted on the heaving surface of the Atlantic for four days and four nights. During the days the sun pursued its course across a cloudless expanse of sky and beat down on the windless ocean and on the lifeboat so fiercely that we came to dread its appearance over the lip of the horizon. The lifeboat—no bigger than *Transcur*—had sixty-five men in it, lying mostly with their feet towards the middle and their heads round the gunwale, like the petals of some macabre flower. A few preferred to squat down on the bottom boards in the centre of the boat where they could see nothing of the world except a frond-like ceiling of criss-crossed legs. Once there, they had to stay, because every inch of boat was taken up by a body reluctant to move. It was hard to move because there was no space which was not already tenanted and because every exposed piece of wood or iron—bolt-heads, the tops of tanks, an old rowlock—was almost red hot to the touch. Each man kept to his own piece of space which he had shaded from the sun with his own body. On the first day the sun began to scorch exposed skin on arms and legs and the bodies of those who were without shirts. The sail was hoisted, only to hang mockingly from its yard and we covered ourselves with the heavy canvas lifeboat cover which protected us from the direct glare of the sun but which raised the temperature under the cover to inferno point. At first the captain encouraged us to row the boat, with three oars on each side, saying that we would soon be picked up and that if we rowed even a few miles to the north-east we might find a breeze. But as the day wore on the men began to calculate the wastage of strength and the loss of precious moisture through trickling sweat and the rowing was abandoned. The crew, even the captain himself, relapsed into torpor —each lying in one position, the body motionless and the mind a blank. I was set to steer which to me was heaven sent relief because the helmsman had more space—about six inches of free space beside him in the pointed stern of the lifeboat. Sometimes there was a light air, enough to give the boat steerage way, but for the most part she was stationary and the sail hung in an ungainly fold. For hour upon hour there was nothing for me to do but to gaze into the water astern and watch the sharks that nuzzled the rudder with their blunt snouts. Occasionally I would flick the tiller so that the sharks sprang to life and raced away for a few yards with a convulsion of their powerful bodies. I never doubted that we would be picked up. I remember looking up at the lifeless sail and being struck by its fascination—making the mind journey forward to some other boat in some other circumstances which I might one day aspire to.

The rain was still drumming onto *Transcur*'s cabin top when I woke early in the morning. I decided to go on straight away, leaving the others to get themselves up and make breakfast at their leisure. I slipped the lines, started the engine and nosed *Transcur* gently out of the basin and into the Canal before the man on the barge had time to come and tell us that we had no right to be there. We soon came out of Rensborg and into the open country once more. With the green wooded banks of the Canal and the rain plopping into the water all round it was for all the world like the River Thames at Oxford or above Maidenhead except for the great ships which continually passed each way. There are no locks in the Kiel Canal except at Brunsbuttel and Kiel at either end and the country the Canal passes through is charming and rural. A few high-level bridges carry roads and railways across it and occasionally one sees a house or a farm. Inevitably, there are men sitting on the banks with fishing lines in patient expectation.

I heard signs of life behind the closed cabin doors and soon Adrian came out to keep me company dressed in his fine new suit of oilskins. A few minutes later a cup of steaming tea was passed out under the door by Patrick's small competent hand. Adrian steered for me with great concentration while I squared up the ropes which I had left lying in heaps on the deck when we slipped from the barge. "Will we be in Denmark to-day?" he asked. "No not to-day but I wouldn't be surprised if we weren't there to-morrow." Denmark was a promised land, an enchanting vision which had always been just beyond the horizon.

We came up with the Holtenau locks at Kiel just before lunch and we were soon inside waiting for the level to go down and the gates into the Baltic to open. Another efficient man from the United Baltic Corporation came on board and we arranged for our duty-free drink and cigarettes and tobacco and a chart to take us up to Sonderborg, to be delivered to the British Kiel Yacht Club which is a few miles outside the gates. Our papers were checked and cleared and we were free to sail the Baltic.

We found the yacht club after asking the way from a fisherman and were soon tied up alongside the jetty. The club might just as easily have been in the Hamble River—with great thoroughness it had been made into a little corner of England, a club house with baths and a bar manned by a cheerful N.C.O. and patronised by aloof and slightly superior army officers sitting on high stools and drinking whisky and soda, calling each other "Sir" and smoking English cigarettes. There was an air of the quaint musty respectability of the English upper class taking their pleasure. "The bar closes at half past two sir" the steward said to me "it opens again at six." The boat club is used by the British Army in Germany who take the club boats out on charter trips to Denmark. Most of the boats are pre-war German yachts which were taken over as reparations—the Germans having now built new ones for themselves. In the afternoon the man from the United Baltic Corporation came with our duty-free parcel. I diffidently offered to pay. "No no" he said "you'll get the bill when you return to England." This, surely, was the Imperial system working to perfection. The United Baltic Corporation did not know us from a bunch of twisters, yet solely on my word, without even a written order, they were happy to pay our Canal dues and to provide us with enough drink to keep us in a state of happy intoxication for weeks. "This is the millennium" Celia said, "we can simply drink until we're inebriates, cruising round Denmark for a month or so and then no doubt come back and get some more—absolutely free." The whole operation was conducted on the basis of trust, without guarantees or bureaucracy of any kind—one of the more acceptable and kindly relics of the past. "If you would just sign the bill sir" was all that was required.

We left Kiel after breakfast the next morning, which was Sunday, and on a bright sunny day without very much wind, sailed up to Sonderborg. We had to use the faithful engine a good bit. *Transcur* was still leaking an unacceptable amount of water and it was quite clear that she would have to be slipped again in Denmark. Celia said, "I'm sure we shall be able to find someone in Sonderborg who will slip her—or at least someone who will know where she can be slipped." Anne said with great confidence, "There'll be one of those cosmopolitan Danes there who will speak English perfectly, and who will arrange the whole thing for us."

We passed into Danish waters in the afternoon and to celebrate it, we stopped the ship and all took off our clothes and plunged into the sea. It was a deep, shimmering, greenish blue with the sun stabbing oblique shafts of light and it was very cold. The boys put on their life jackets and spluttered and splashed about in the water close to *Transcur* with ropes round them. Later in the afternoon we saw the shore ahead of us and soon the wooded fairy tale land that we expected of Denmark began to take shape. As we got closer to the land we saw the romantic beech woods sweeping gracefully down to the water's edge and then the Castle that guards the entrance to Sonderborg came in sight. We followed a fishing boat round the point and into the fine big harbour and we tied up alongside the quay beside a German motor yacht.

The boys ran off ashore in great excitement to see if they could hear anyone speaking Danish and soon Celia and Anne and I followed them and walked into the town. The boys had been promised a special present when we reached Denmark and although the shops were closed they made their dispositions for the next day—Adrian wanted a fishing rod and Patrick a very splendid German car. Then we took them to a café which turned out to be something of a night club with a band and people dancing and they managed to keep themselves awake for long enough to eat vast ice cream cakes and gaze with round eyes at the peculiar and fascinating things that grown-ups did when boys were asleep in their beds. We took them back along the fairy-lit quay to where *Transcur* was lying and tumbled them into their bunks. Patrick stretched himself out in his sleeping bag and yawned a last good night "If this is Denmark it's a smashing place."

Chapter Fifteen

We all slept peacefully and soundly on our first night in Denmark, the boat suffused with an atmosphere of contentment, only punctuated by the occasional snore. We woke up happy and refreshed on Monday morning. There was a sense of achievement in having reached the promised land after so many difficulties and misfortunes and we were in that halcyon state, which lasts for no more than a day or so, when we have reached our destination and have not yet begun to worry about the return trip. Two weeks and two days of our precious five weeks had been used and we felt inclined to take things easy, at least for a few days. But we could not quite relax completely because we knew that before attempting any further serious trips *Transcur* would have to be made at least reasonably water-tight. Certainly, Denmark should be the best place in the world for this to be done cheaply and efficiently but there was always the nagging fear that the boat had suffered something more than superficial damage—something that just could not be mended quickly—and that she would need a major overhaul before she could be made seaworthy. We knew that when we eventually got back home she would have to be taken to Mr. Drake or to someone else who understood old smacks, to be done up properly. Then, there would be no language difficulty, no time limit and everything would be easier. The Welmerlegen yard had done their best and they had succeeded in making it possible for us to continue the passage but still, there was a big leak somewhere which ought to be cured before we attempted the return trip across the North Sea.

On the credit side, Celia's leg had miraculously got better. I asked about it at breakfast and she said "The rough treatment must have done it good. It hardly hurts at all and it doesn't keep me awake at night."

We all went ashore and spent the morning shopping, changing money, drinking beer and eating smorrebrod. We visited the toy shop and the boys were bought their long promised presents. No boys deserved a treat more than these two. They had put up with all the dangers and discomforts without a single word of complaint and they had shown a quite remarkable capacity to enjoy themselves and be cheerful in adverse circumstances.

The people we met in the shops and along the quay were charming and helpful and we saw at once from the atmosphere of the town that we had come to a friendly, pleasant country. The big harbour was full of activity and interest and the boys played happily among the fishing boats and yachts that lay alongside. We cleared the Immigration and Customs, had our passports stamped and then Celia and I went off to have a drink by ourselves and to find Anne's cosmopolitan Dane. "Don't worry", she said "you'll certainly find him without any trouble." "All right" Celia said "we'll try the yachts in the harbour first". We went and had a beer at the little pub opposite our berth and then we walked slowly round the harbour scrutinizing all the twenty odd boats that lay alongside. Most of them were German, a few were Dutch and there were no more than half a dozen Danish yachts. We went on board a big ketch, all shining and new, but the owner and his family spoke no English and we found it quite impossible to make ourselves understood. We held an amiable but abortive conversation in sign language, accepted a beer and a smorrebrod and went ashore again baffled.

At the very end of the quay there was a modern yacht with a Danish ensign and a tall man was standing in the cockpit splicing a rope. It was quite clear from the appearance of the boat that the tall Dane kept her in first-class order and had all the expertise of a real seaman. "Here's our man, or rather Anne's man" Celia said.

As soon as he saw us he smiled broadly "Hello there" he said in English with a hint of an American accent overlaying the Danish, "You must be from the English yacht. Come on board and have a drink." Celia and I looked at each other, shrugged our shoulders and climbed on board where we were introduced to his American wife and his young son. Anne's prognosis had been quite correct but not so surprising as all that when one came to think about it. The cosmopolitan Dane is a clearly defined type who can be found in most parts of the world, usually round harbours and docks, so why not in Denmark itself? The cosmopolitan Dane is invariably completely integrated with the country he happens to be in—unlike the English abroad who become more and more English the longer they stay. The Dane speaks the language perfectly with a characteristic sing-song accent, quite unmistakable regardless of the country. He is often in a high position in business or industry. The Danes above all other races have the facility to live and prosper in foreign countries without becoming objects of envy, ridicule or hatred.

Oskar lived with his family in America and was on a holiday sailing in his home waters. He had seen *Transcur* come in the previous evening "She looks like a good tough old boat" he said. We told him about our troubles and at once he agreed to help us find a boat yard who would slip *Transcur* and do some more temporary caulking. "There's quite a good yard here" he said "on the other side of the harbour. We'll go over and see if he can help." We all went across the harbour in *Transcur*'s dinghy but we found that a fishing boat was already hauled out on the slip for repair and the yard would not be able to take *Transcur* for four or five days. Oskar asked the owner of the yard to suggest an alternative. There was a long conversation in Danish and then Oskar and I rowed back across the harbour to the main hotel in the town and Oskar put through a call to Faaborg, which is on the island of Funen about twenty-five miles away.

162

After a long conversation Oskar said "If you can be there by to-morrow afternoon, he will put you on the slip on Wednesday morning and do the job straight away." We went back to *Transcur* and told Anne that we had found her cosmopolitan Dane and that everything had been arranged. In the evening we all went to the Continental Bar on the quay and drank beer and schnapps until we became maudlin and slightly morose. I was full of self-reproach, which is near to self-pity and which is brought on violently by the schnapps, and the whole dreary catalogue had to be repeated. It was a hopeless mess we found ourselves in, five hundred miles from home in a leaky old boat. The girls tried to cheer me up but with every schnapps I sank deeper into gloom and despondency until the barman threw us out and we rolled rhythmically back to the quay.

A young couple were standing on the quay gazing at *Transcur*. "A fine old boat" the young man said "You have made a good passage from England? How we would like to have a boat like that." And then I felt better. We sailed out of Sonderborg early next morning, past the Castle and out to the tip of Als close along the alluring, wooded shore. It was a soft, friendly coast-line with trees everywhere and tidy farms chequering the country-side with their neat symmetry. At the tip of Als we struck out across the Lille Baelt, a moderate northerly breeze hurrying us across to the lighthouse on the northern point of Aero, and thence into a complicated winding channel through small islands into the approaches to Faaborg. There were no tides to give a set, no dangerous rocks or treacherous shoals and the buoys and marks were all clearly shown on the chart we had bought in Sonderborg.

We came up with the town of Faaborg in the afternoon, found our boat yard and tied up comfortably alongside a wooden staging. One of the boat yard workers—he told us he had been to sea in the British Merchant Navy—acted as our interpreter and introduced us to three Danes who, he said, would mend our boat. They were huge men, like Vikings, only lacking horned helmets. The yard was old and the gear and equipment although obviously very efficient, seemed primitive. It was a simple matter

163

to throw one's mind back a few centuries and imagine these same Danes building their longships and setting off to spread terror along the seaboards of France and England. It was arranged that *Transcur* would be hauled on the tiny slip at eight the following morning. On our way ashore to explore the town and have our supper, we saw a fine big wooden fishing boat, nearing completion in the yard and this gave us great hope that a good job would be made of *Transcur*.

Promptly as arranged the next day *Transcur* was hauled up on the slip, the winch which was driven by an ancient engine creaking and shuddering as she emerged slowly from the water. The three Danes set about her at once with big caulking mallets, ramming in cotton wherever the seams appeared weak, while I searched about under the bottom for bad places, a drill which by now I had perfected. In the afternoon they shrugged their shoulders, said they could do no more, and slid *Transcur* back into the water. The bill for their day's work and for the use of their slip was no more than five pounds.

Celia and I peered into the pump well under the cabin floor— another ritual we had become accustomed to. We did not have to wait long before we saw the tell-tale trickle of water running quickly through the bilge. It was impossible to see exactly where the water was coming from because of the accommodation built up from the bilge inside, and because of what remained of the inner lining, originally put into the boat to carry the cargo. The cement between the frames made it even more difficult to see exactly where the water was coming from. "If there was only one big leak", Celia said "we could find it and stop it. The trouble is you can't actually see the water coming in fast at any one place." Feeling miserably depressed, we decided to take *Transcur* out, although it was now well on in the afternoon, to see how much water she made when under way. There was a smart northerly breeze, and after a quick look at the chart, we decided to go on to Aeroskobing. "If we get away now", I said "we'll be in by nightfall. It's only seventeen miles and we shall make good at least six knots in this breeze." Anne and the children had been ashore for a swim and a walk in the town and as

164

soon as they came back we got under way. "We won't pump either until the water comes over the cabin floor, or until we reach Aeroskobing", I said, "we'll just see what happens first."

We waved good-bye to the friendly Danes and set off. They had done the best they could but they had not been given time to make a thorough job. If she could have been kept on the slip for a week and the job done slowly and methodically they would probably have made her strong and tight but in the course of one day it was asking a lot of them. On the face of it, they seemed to have made her worse than she had been before. As soon as we were clear of the harbour we hoisted sail and the breeze took us in charge, blowing fresh on our quarter and pushing *Transcur* along at something near her maximum speed. The sun shone and the little Baltic waves were whipped up into a gay dance as we twisted our way through the winding Faaborg channel and sailed out into the Lille Baelt. This time, we left the long thin island of Aero to starboard and shot down between it and the many small islands off the coast of Funen. The sun picked out the slopes of the island in a riot of colour emphasising its gentle contours. Scarlet roofs against the bright green fields— the darker greens and browns of the trees with a ribbon of white sand between them and the deep blue sea.

Transcur, perversely, seemed to be on top of her form, rushing carelessly through the steep little seas, whisking off their tops and hurling them out to leeward and then pushing the next wave with the tip of her bowsprit. The sails pulled strong and true and with a line round the tiller she kept straight on her course as if she was doing her very best to make the harbour before the tell-tale line of water appeared over the cabin floor. We picked up the point of land called Urehoved Flak and came flying in close to the coast until we saw the outer buoy of the Aeroskobing entrance. Then we gybed *Transcur* round in a smother of spray and stood towards the little town with its twin piers chalk white in the evening light. Anne said quietly "I'm afraid she's lost this little wager with herself. The water's over the floor." And she switched on the electric pump just before

165

we raced through the tiny entrance to the harbour, rounded smartly up inside and clawed the sails down as fast as we could, Patrick and Adrian helping to get the wind out of them and still their effort with secure rope tiers. With our way still on we slid alongside an empty space at the quay.

Aeroskobing is a serene harbour in a pretty setting—surely copied from a picture postcard of a traditional Danish harbour—with the town clustered round and spilling over the gentle slopes behind. It was blowing hard by the time we got past the piers and between the high harbour walls. We felt a sudden hush of stillness and peace after the bluster outside. There were the usual handful of German yachts lying alongside and one English, from the Kiel Canal Club, as well as a steamer and the ferry over from Svendborg. But what riveted our attention and set us glancing at one another was an orderly looking boat yard with a good slip on which was a yacht, by the looks of her, ready to be put back in the water. We all went ashore before dark and walked up through the town, pausing to look at this boat yard which was deserted but open for anyone to walk through. There was a big wooden fishing boat like the one at Faaborg in process of construction and we could see her stout planking fastened to massive and closely spaced frames. It was clear that they knew how to build wooden boats in this country, but whether their outlook would be sympathetic towards an old English smack remained to be seen. "I'll go and see this man first thing in the morning." Aeroskobing—quite unspoilt—was an example of a seventeenth century Danish town. Narrow cobbled streets and timber framed houses jostling one another, the plaster of the houses painted in characteristic red. There was a park near the harbour with formal flower beds and statues as well as a wild part where the boys at once went to earth. As in Faaborg the night life was hard to find and all the town could rise to was a couple of beers at the hotel. Before we went to bed we shifted *Transcur* to the windward side of the harbour where she would ride quietly in the now gale force wind and we went to bed depressed about the leaks and worried about the outcome of the trip. *Transcur* had almost filled her bilges with water again from the time we passed the harbour entrance to when we went to bed—not good enough for the North Sea.

The proprietor of the boat yard was an elderly, gentle Dane with a soft voice and a kind manner; a man one could like instantly. He spoke enough English to be able to understand the gist of what had happened to us and he listened attentively and with obvious interest when Celia and I explained our predicament to him. "We'll haul your boat out if you want us to", he said "and we will do our best. But I do not promise that we shall stop your leak. By what you have told me your boat is in need of a lot of work, and we have not the time. However, bring her to the slip tomorrow morning at seven o'clock and we will do our best," he repeated. The situation seemed suddenly more hopeful than it had at any time since the Terschelling bank. "That man gives me confidence" Celia said "I really think that this time they'll do the old boat a bit of good." Both Celia and I have always suffered from alternate moods of optimism and black despair when it comes to anything concerning our boats. In all our difficulties if the mood has been right, we have seized on any twig of hope and identified it with our complete salvation and if the mood has been wrong, we have quickly descended into the very deepest despondency. We know, really, that this is an unbalanced view of life—in the long run one gets more or less what one deserves, sometimes a little more, sometimes a little less, but it averages out in the end.

We had a day off from worry in Aeroskobing. We took the boys and went for a trip in a bus across the island of Aero. The island was full of friendly charm that we had come to expect of Denmark; the boys were delighted with the postal system which appeared to be operated entirely by the bus driver who stopped anywhere to collet or deliver letters. The countryside was as neat and trim and prosperous as one is led to expect of Denmark and everyone we saw wore the unmistakable look of easy contentment that comes from a life unharassed by commercial pressures. It is a look that is fast disappearing—particularly in England—where the constant urge for bigger and finer material trappings overlays rustic charm and tranquility. Everyone in the bus talked at and about the two little English boys and made a great fuss of them. At Marstal we went for a swim from an indifferent stony beach and wandered through the town until we came to the Ship Museum. It was closed—we were just too late to go in. But an old man came out of the little house opposite and said that if we wanted to see the Museum he would fetch Captain Hansen. He set off up the street at a cracking pace and soon Captain Hansen himself arrived on his bicycle and opened the Museum with a big iron key. He was an enthusiast on his subject and talked to us for an hour in his fluent, yet slightly broken English, about his ship models and about his experiences. He had been captain in sailing ships and steamers and had been as familiar with the sea ports of the world as he was now with his magnificent models. The Marstal Ship Yard had once been specialists in careening the big sailing ships of the seventeenth century and Captain Hansen had preserved old capstans, massive blocks and all the complicated gear that had been used for this work. When we had seen his Museum he was as pleased to have shown it to us as we were to have seen it and we all shook hands with him warmly.

Back at Aeroskobing in the bus it was late and the boys went to bed after one last look at their jungle hide-out in the park. Anne and I went ashore in another vain search for the gay life of Denmark. We managed to get only mildly tight by keeping the proprietor of the hotel out of his bed until nearly ten o'clock at which time he made it clear to us that he thought all honest people should be at home. Anne and I walked round the harbour wall watching the moon throw a brilliant path of light across the smooth sea and over the sleeping town.

The next morning *Transcur* was hauled smoothly onto the slip by a quiet electric motor and two men immediately started work on the bottom. They shook their heads sadly over the depredations of both the Welmerlegen and the Faaborg yards and started to search systematically for weak places in the calking. They found a number of places to be re-caulked and they produced some strips of lead coated with a very sticky bituminous compound which they nailed over a few of the worst seams. I went

168

round after them, stopping over their caulking with Seelastic for lack of a more suitable material. The only stopping compound they had themselves, it appeared, would be useless unless the boat had a week on the slip to dry out thoroughly but they were confident that their treatment would stop most of the leaks, at least temporarily. Patrick and Adrian played in the park all the morning and after lunch Celia and Anne took them off for a swim at a nearby beach. At tea time the job was more or less done. In any case *Transcur* had to be launched because the slip was wanted for another boat the next day. We put her back in her berth against the outer wall of the harbour and in due course our friend the proprietor of the yard came round and presented me with his bill. It was for five pounds ten. The Danish yards, and the Welmerlegen Ship Yard if it comes to that, were very fair with us over their charges and made not the slightest attempt to exploit or overcharge us in any way. You could travel the length and breadth of England and never find a yard to slip *Transcur* for five pounds, yet the Danish yards not only slipped her but also did the work for this sum. In fact they must have charged nothing for the actual slipping because we worked it out that the five pounds would have been amply taken up by the men's time and materials alone. We obviously did not look like the sort of yachtsmen who could afford to pay through the nose and, seeing us in difficulties, they kindly adjusted their charges accordingly. "We have done our best" the proprietor said, "I hope she will be all right until you get back to England."

He had certainly done well, because when we looked in the bilges, for the first time since Terschelling there was no significant amount of water running into the pump well. "Go carefully in the North Sea" he said, "she may leak more in a rough sea". We paid his bill and assured him that we would be careful in the North Sea although how one was to take care in the North Sea was not clear to me. If you are in the North Sea you are in it, go you so carefully as you may.

Chapter Sixteen

"Let's just not worry about the leaks any more" Celia said. "We've done our best to be rid of them and if there are a few left, well, we shall just have to learn to live with them as happily as may be." "All right, we'll forget about the goddamm leaks." I said "I quite agree, I've had enough of them as well. As long as the old boat holds body and soul together until we get home, we'll let the insurance company worry about the leaks".

"As far as I can see" Anne said with her usual logic "we don't have to worry too much. After all, it's not as if we have to pump the bilge ourselves, the electric motor does it for us and it seems to be just as keen as ever." "All right, to hell with the leaks" I toasted and we all swilled a large schnapps. Anne was right about the pump. It is compact, highly efficient and takes a very small amount of current from our battery. It is a mystery to me why electric bilge pumps are not more widely used and why ocean sailers do not as a rule carry one. There is no single piece of equipment on board that has served us better. Without it, *Transcur* would most certainly have foundered on the Terschelling bank and even if she had not, it would have been next to impossible to have sailed back to harbour and at the same time to have pumped continuously with the Vortex pump, single handed. There is nothing in the world like pumping bilges to drain the energy and the spirit out of a man.

Now, we had to decide on our programme for what remained of our holiday. It was already August fifteenth and come what may we had to be back in England, somewhere within train-ride of London, by Sunday August thirtieth because both Anne and I were due back at work on the first day of September. Clearly, it would be best to get right back to Bradwell by August twenty-ninth at the latest, leaving us a day to wash the salt out of our hair and get ourselves into a mental state for that other life which we had left, it seemed years ago, and which we had quite forgotten about. We were already five hundred miles away from home and would be further still in another few days and we calculated that we should leave at least ten days for the return trip. This put Copenhagen out of the picture, to the disappointment of us all. There would be no Tivoli gardens, no drinking in the Nyhavn. We would have to be content with South Denmark—Funen, Aero and Langeland, pleasant enough from what we had seen so far.

The next day we sailed out of Aeroskobing with a light northerly breeze to send us past the little island of St. Egholm and then into a narrow, winding but beautifully marked channel between the shallow banks of Birkholm and Bedholm. The channel became so winding that it was hard to distinguish between the port and starboard hand marks but soon we came out of it and into a lovely open piece of water almost surrounded by the two islands of Langeland and Stryno. Langeland is a thin island over thirty miles long and for most of its length not more than three or four miles wide. We had picked on Lohals, a small town at the top of the island, as the furthest point we would be able to reach. After we got to Lohals, we would have to turn round and begin to make our way back home. The scenery in this part of Denmark is like the people—good to look at, neat, clean and well ordered. Occasionally there is an outbreak of grandeur when one comes upon some fine point of land jutting nobly into the sea with a thick covering of tall, elegant beech trees crowding one another

171

to the water's edge as if they only wanted to leap off and strike across the sea to the next island.

As we sailed up the coast of Langeland the wind went round to the north-west so that it was blowing straight on to the shore. We picked up the marks of a channel that led us close into the beach for a couple of miles and then soon we saw the town and the harbour of Lohals. By now the wind had freshened. A nasty short sea was running and we could see the vicious little waves breaking against the shore to leeward of us and hurling spray high up onto the rocks. We passed through the narrowest part of the channel, no more than two hundred yards from the beach, and when we came up with the harbour we sailed off-shore for half a mile and then brought *Transcur* into the wind. She pitched violently while we took down the sails so that it was difficult to keep a foothold on deck and Celia held her into the wind's eye with the engine running hard while I dropped the wildly flapping foresail, pulled the mainsail down and lashed it along the boom. "All, right, turn her round and we'll run in."

Transcur rolled heavily as she turned and then she ran fast down wind towards the harbour with the engine ticking over as slowly as it would go. The windage in the mast and rigging gave her more speed than we would have liked but there was no other way to approach the harbour as it lay in a little indentation in the coast and the wind was blowing straight into it. We could see the two piers which formed the entrance and the superstructure of a large ferry which seemed to be moored just inside. "I don't see how we're going to get in" Anne said, "as far as I can see that ferry's completely blocking the entrance." "It'll open out when we get down to it" I said confidently. As we came nearer it did seem that the ferry was blocking the entrance but we could not be sure until suddenly we brought the two piers abeam and saw that the ferry lay right across from one side to the other, completely filling the gap so that not even a rowing boat could get through. Suddenly we were in trouble. There was now no room to turn and so I slammed the engine into reverse and opened the throttle so that it roared and spluttered and shook

172

as the seas lifted *Transcur's* stern and her propeller began to race. There was no room either to starboard or to port and *Transcur* was still going towards the shore not thirty yards away, in spite of the engine, under the force of the wind behind her. Then Patrick shouted from the cabin, "Daddy, the engine's on fire" and I saw that clouds of black smoke and fumes were billowing out of the alleyway. I raced forward shouting to Celia, "Turn the engine off at once and get the extinguisher". I struggled to clear away the anchor striving not to fumble in my anxiety and hurled it over, letting out chain feverishly "By Christ, you must hold, you must hold."

When I looked up the shore was racing towards us. I glanced over towards the ferry, sitting smugly between the piers and saw a man gesticulating wildly on the jetty. For a moment it looked as though *Transcur* would be dashed to pieces on the rocks. Celia had brought the children into the cockpit and Anne had somehow managed to grab life jackets. Then the anchor bit into the ground, the chain became taut with a bang and she pivoted round and stopped—with her stern no more than yards from the rocks. We could hear the surf crashing against the shore and then drawing itself back with a gruesome sucking sound like the breathing of some giant creature, as it gathered itself for the next fling. Anne came and helped me tear off the sail tiers and when they were half off I hauled on the main halliard and pulled the sail up as fast as I could hand over hand. "Break out the jib", I shouted "on the starboard side. Tiller hard to starboard".

Patrick, with his quick intelligence, let go the tripping line and as Celia pulled on the jib sheet the sail unrolled and I grabbed it by the sheet and held it to windward. *Transcur's* bow slowly payed off, the mainsail filled and she began to gather way. As she moved ahead Anne and I pulled in the slack on the anchor chain. "If she won't sail it out" I shouted "we'll have to slip the cable. Go down into the chain locker now and cut the lashing on the last link. You'll see it tied up round the samson post." Slowly *Transcur* came up with her anchor and when she was over it there was an instant when the chain came bar tight and I thought she wouldn't do it, but her great weight stood her well

173

and suddenly she sailed the anchor out, the chain came slack, and I was able to haul it in. Celia eased the helm and changed over the jib as she gathered her way and suddenly we were safe, almost in open water and she was sailing hard to windward with her lee rail a smother of spray, clawing her way off the land towards safety. The mainsail was only two-thirds hoisted and the deck was a mess of ropes and chain. I squared up, hoisted the mainsail properly, and went aft to look at the engine. "That was a near one" Celia said "my nerves didn't like that much." "Nor mine neither." Anne emerged from the chain locker having cut the lashing round the samson post, "Is that one over now?" she asked.

I saw at once what had gone wrong with the engine, which had not in fact been on fire at all. As soon as Celia had turned it off the smoking had stopped and she had not used the extinguisher. The trouble had been caused by vibration which had shaken the circulating water cock from the vertical into the horizontal position, cutting off the cooling water to the engine which had at once begun to run hot. The black smoke had come from the charring cylinder head gasket and escaping oil fumes. It was still almost red hot but it had not seized up and I hoped it would be all right when it cooled. We set the foresail and started to beat to windward across the strait towards Lundeborg, on the other side. When we were half way across Patrick pointed aft to Lohals "Look, the sitting duck's gone. We can go in after all."

Everyone made a fuss of *Transcur* in Lohals. The harbour master came in his fine uniform with a retinue of helpers and small boys, a space was made for us alongside the quay and we were berthed with ceremony. The harbourmaster had enough English to offer some apology for the presence of the sitting duck and he drank a whisky in the cabin as we paid our four kroner harbour dues—the only dues we were ever charged in Denmark.

Lohals was as unspoilt as we had been led to believe from the tourist books. We walked through the noble forest with the sky far away above and the rustle of the leaves and branches blending with the mutter of the sea against the rocks. We wondered if in

174

Transcur we had ever been in a lovelier place. There was a charm and a romance about the tall forest which was new to us—a cottage deep in the trees with a pretty blonde girl at the gate, a cut down narrow twisting paths to the shore at the very tip of the island. The boys took their clothes off and ran wildly in and out of the sea screaming their pleasure into the crisp morning air while we sat and threw stones into a still sea pool among the rocks. The sun turned the sea deep blue. Anne wandered off in search of wild flowers leaving Celia and me to sit and drink in the peace. This was the high peak of our journey—worth every bit of the travail. The day was one of idle pleasure, a rest before what might be an arduous passage home.

Next day we waved good-bye to the brassbound harbourmaster and made a slow passage down to the corner of Thuro in a light air. Then the wind left us and it began to rain hard and steadily as we motored up the long, winding and intensely beautiful approach channel to Svendborg. The channel is narrow with steep wooded banks studded with the mansions and chalets of the Danish rich—green lawns sweeping down to charming boat houses, baroque turrets commanding views of the lovely waterway. The town to us was uninteresting—probably because of the rain—and we wandered through it for an hour or so buying a new glass for our cabin lamp and toy boats for the boys. We decided to push on and get out of the city and into the quiet harbours again, where we are happier. The way out from Svendborg to the west was almost as lovely as the channel to the eastward and a little breeze came to help us along. The rain cleared away and we were able to follow the narrow channel through to Drejo. We passed the square rigged brigantine *Lille Dan* lying at anchor, apparently with no one on board, as bright and smart as could be in her red paint—the colours of the Danish shipping line of Lauritzeu to whom she belongs. Soby was the only port we could make that night because Aeroskobing was to windward and in any case Soby had the attraction of being a new place and on our way back to Kiel.

The wind freshened as we came clear of the land and *Transcur* put on her best speed and raced across the strait towards Soby.

175

There would have been enough wind for a couple of reefs if it had not been fair on the quarter, and as the glass was high, the sky fine and we were approaching a weather shore I let her run at her full speed. To our great pleasure she did not make too much water although she was heeled over and straining considerably and in an hour she had covered the distance. As we came into the lee of the dark land the wind eased and we saw the lights of Soby. Anne and I took the sails down and we motored cautiously into the tiny harbour and tied alongside. Soby was to be our last port in Denmark. We counted through our money and found that we had enough to buy Celia a Danish sweater and myself a pair of trousers, well and strongly made at a reasonable price. The little town was very charming and the boys were able to run about the streets and play on the beach without our worrying about them. It seemed a great waste of effort to have fought our way to Denmark and then to find it necessary to leave again after so brief a stay and before we had seen the best part of the country. Why go back? No confusion would be caused by my absence that could not be put right by a few deft arrangements. The boys would miss school, but what could be better for them than a cruise in foreign lands? If we simply stayed on, abandoning our responsibilities the worst that would happen to us would be a money shortage. In due course we would have exhausted all that we could persuade people in London to send us. But I reckoned, as we sat with our schnapps in a little bar overlooking the harbour, that it ought to be possible to find some gainful occupation in Scandinavia to keep us going. Celia said, "The time seems to have suddenly all gone and now we're in a hurry again. Back to normal I suppose."

We left Denmark before lunch and watched Soby disappearing astern of us with regret. "We must come back here again" Anne said. The wind was moderate from the south-east which gave us a fast run up to the top corner of Aero but which was right ahead of us as soon as we rounded the lighthouse and set our course for Kiel once more. The distance from Soby to Holtenau, the entrance to the Kiel Canal, is only forty odd miles but I didn't expect to get in much before daylight the next day with the wind uncertain in strength and ahead of us. In fact it eased once we rounded the lighthouse on the tip of Aero and we tacked on and off shore the whole afternoon, making slow progress down the long but very pretty coast of the island. At seven o'clock I was able to get good cross bearings off the southern tip of Aero and to fix a position from which to make a departure for Holtenau. Then mist came down and the wind became fluky and variable in direction.

Celia read a story to the boys for half an hour and they went to bed contented enough with their day—a good run ashore in the morning and setting off on a passage in the afternoon which they always enjoy. The mist continued into the night and with the constant alterations of course due to shifting wind and our slow progress, I became uncertain of our position to within a few miles. As the entrance to the Kiel fjord is not more than a couple of miles across I was uneasy. I had expected to see buoys and a lot of shipping going in and out of Kiel but there was nothing but black night and thin uneven mist. Some time after midnight the mist cleared and we saw lights on the shore ahead of us but none that we could identify with our chart and no sign of the Kiel light vessel. Celia stared into the darkness and kept a look out for any light that could be identified while I pored over the chart and the pilot book. My eyes began to water with the strain of gazing at the navigation books in the poor light— only a dimned oil lamp so that Celia would not be dazzled in the cockpit. As I stood in the alleyway propped comfortably against the bulkhead, I lazily allowed my attention to wander round the familiar objects. The switchboard with the engine controls and the accommodation light switches, the galley with the fat complacent kettle sitting on top of the stove, Adrian's toy boat on the quarter berth throwing a deep shadow onto the bulkhead, the binoculars on their rack like twin bottles of liqueur brandy, the shining brass clock on its varnished board and next to it the barometer. We had bought these twins years back in *Santa Lucia* days. They had looked very grand and businesslike screwed on to the inside of her coach roof. Then I looked at the barometer again—surely not—it had dropped nearly half an inch in the last couple of hours. I gave it a tap and the black needle moved with a jerk downwards again. I went into the cockpit and looked at the sky, dark overhead but black to windward. "It's going to blow" I said to Celia.

We were now getting quite close to the shore and still we could not decided on our position. I knew it was going to blow and I knew it was essential to find out exactly where we were before the wind came. Celia said "I think we ought to take the mainsail down until we find out where we are. We don't want to stand on towards the shore in the dark." This was sense. For all I could tell we might be to the eastward or to the west of the Kiel light vessel and in any case I knew the sail would have to be reefed and it would be just as well to take it down and make a neat job of it now. I let go the halliard, lowered the sail and left it lying over the cabin top in a depressing heap while Celia and I scanned the maze of shore lights for something familiar. Then Celia saw the loom of a flashing light far up to windward. Surely it must be the Kiel light—I counted the flashes with the stop watch—yes it is the Kiel light. Thank God for that anyway. There was another flashing light on the Schleswig Holstein shore, whose characteristics were not clear from our German chart but bearings of these two showed that we had been carried far to leeward, presumably by a current that I had found no mention of in the sailing directions. By that reckoning we were a good ten miles to the east of the entrance to the Kiel fjord. While the sail was down I put a reef in it although the wind was still only moderate and then we got under way again and prepared ourselves for a long beat to windward before we could make the shelter of the Kiel fjord. "Better make some coffee" I said to Celia "Half past three. It'll be light soon."

We hadn't swallowed our coffee before the wind came—first in little extra puffs laying themselves on top of the moderate breeze until they turned it into a fresh breeze and then building up inexorably from fresh to strong. *Transcur* lay over and began to creak and groan and bury her bows into the steep little seas sending the spray flying aft, the sheets pinned in and the luff of the mainsail lifting in the gusts. "We'll roll up the jib first, then

178

take another reef in the mainsail, then change to the smaller jib". "Hold on tight" Celia said as I went forward with the safety harness buckled round my chest. It would never do to fall overboard on such a night. Celia luffed the wind out of the mainsail as I eased the halliard, pulled down the luff of the sail and tied in the cringle of the third reef. Then the reefing tackle under the boom had to be taken off the first reef cringle and hooked to the third. Celia eased the sheet and let *Transcur* pay off a bit to take some of the weight out of the sail while I heaved the cringle down and made it fast. How I blessed our loose footed sail as I tied up the points and saw how neat and snug it set. It was an easy job to pull down the jib, already furled into a long sausage by the Wickham Martin gear, haul the bowsprit traveller in, unhook the sail and unshackle the sheet. By the time it was done it was almost daylight and the iron line of the horizon was beginning to show under a black starless sky. I brought the jib back to the cockpit and stuffed it into the quarter berth. "Well done" Celia said. "It's blowing harder now but she's lying quite easy". She was quiet, but she wasn't making much progress against the wind with the imbalance of her partly reefed sails. "She needs the small jib and the foresail to be reefed." I went through the cabin to the fo'c'sle, past Anne apparently sleeping peacefully in the lee bunk although I guessed she must have been woken by the noise of my feet on the deck above, and would be up and fully conscious in a few moments if we needed her help. As soon as I slid open the fo'c'sle door to get the storm jib from the rack by Patrick's head I saw him in the half light clinging instinctively to the side of his bunk to keep himself from falling out, his face to the ships' side and his back wedged against the rope support of his pipe cot. There was much more noise in the fo'c'sle than in the saloon, with heavy spray falling on the deck above, the crashes and bumps as the bow hit the steep solid seas and rhythmical swing and knocks of the bundles of shackles and gear hanging round the fo'c'sle beam shelf as *Transcur*'s bows slowly lifted and then fell suddenly away into the next trough. I had to crawl along the sail rack right forward past his peacefully sleeping face to get the jib, but he did not stir. Any noise made by me was

179

drowned in the natural cacophony of the fo'c'sle. It was as if he was sleeping inside the big drum during the last movement of the Eroica.

I shut the door and came aft with the sail, pausing in the alleyway to switch on the electric pump. "Reach in and switch it off when you hear it suck air" I said to Celia. Then I went forward again and set the tiny storm jib, pulling it out just over half way along the bowsprit and sweating it up tight on the halliard. It isn't an easy job in a rough sea. You have to get right up in the very eyes of the ship, in the tiny triangle of space forward of the dinghy, to hook the foot of the jib onto the traveller. Even though practically hove-to *Transcur* was dipping her bows so that green water came tumbling over every few moments, making it wet and un-nerving and causing me to feel for the reassuring life line. Once the sail is hooked on and hauled out along the bowsprit the wind catches it and it bangs and threshes about wildly until you can get aft to the halliard and haul it up tight, when the sail suddenly transforms itself from a demon to a tractable and helpful creature. While I was on the fore deck I reefed the foresail for good measure and when I finally stood by the shrouds and looked at *Transcur* bravely struggling against the wind with her cut down rig she seemed to me to be solid and capable and safe.

The first of the day was slowly spreading over the confused sea, showing a vista of breaking waves, the crests dragged off the tops by the wind and hurled down to make white bubbly webs over the green bulk of the water. Everything looked close and unreal in the mellow early morning light, the sails and ropes and wires glistening with a million pearls of spray which clung tenuously to them until the wind tore them away and sent them stinging across the deck to leeward. Celia sat in the cockpit clasping the tiller and looking at the compass, her face dark with concern and her hair streaming away in lank wet tails. A big sea crashed against *Transcur*'s side just where I was standing, sending a white sheet of spray straight across the cockpit to catch her full on the side of the face so that she winced and turned away for a second. I knew that the cold water would have found its

180

way under her oilskin coat and would be making a tortuous journey in icy rivulets down inside her jersey to lie in a clammy pool somewhere round her waist. Not every girl's cup of tea this sort of thing, I reflected.

Transcur picked up speed with the jib set. I went aft and hauled the main sheet in tight and she began to make steady progress to windward. The wind had veered half a point and had freshened to gale force and now she was heading almost directly for the light which we could see clearly ahead and slightly to windward. She was heeling over about as much as she ever does heel over which is twenty-five degrees, and was moving fast up to windward under her snug reefs. She was making a fair bit of water; Celia had kept the pump going all the time I had been changing the sails and it was only now sucking air. "Once we get up to the light vessel we should be able to bear away and run up the fjord, then we shall soon be in." "The sooner the better if you ask me. Doesn't she go well with her reefs! If only she wasn't leaking it would be perfect." Then we saw Patrick in the companionway. "What's happening? There's a terrific noise in the fo'c'sle and there was a drip in my ear. Oh I see," he added "it's blowing a gale." I steered while Celia went below and got herself reasonably dry. Patrick came to the companionway when he was dressed, to talk as he likes to do in the early morning at sea. "You stand there and work the pump" I said "Switch it on every ten minutes and leave it going till it sucks." This was a fine job for Patrick. He liked to be allowed to work the pump and to be able to do so every ten minutes was a real treat.

Transcur was easy enough to steer. With a line passed over the tiller and back round the boom crutch stanchion you could sit out of the wind on the lee side of the cockpit and control her without difficulty. The wind and the seas had got up remarkably quickly and I guessed the blow would not last long. *Transcur* was making very good progress in view of the strength of the wind, which seemed to be increasing, and the steepness of the seas, which were so close together that she had no chance to ride over them but simply hit them with all her weight so that the deck and the cockpit were constantly swept by spray. This, after all,

181

was the sort of weather she had been designed to deal with all those years ago and it was not surprising that she did it so well. The gear all seemed strong and sound and nothing showed any sign of strain. Our only anxiety was the leak which although big, seemed to be constant.

Patrick stood faithfully by the pump and switched it on for two minutes in every ten. The light vessel gradually came nearer and grew more distinct. Anne was up and making scrambled egg with some difficulty but great expertise and Adrian was playing with cars on the cabin floor. It was dry inside and much quieter than in the cockpit. I began to see a few ships converging on the light vessel, all from further to the north. Celia came and steered while I ate my scrambled egg, drank hot coffee and felt the goodness of it spread through my whole being so that I forgot that I had been up all night and was tired. It was clear that we were being set in towards the shore which was now quite close. "Hurry up and get the breakfast washed up and put away" I said to Celia "and we'll go about and take a leg out to seaward. Then we shall fetch the light vessel. We'll be able to bear away a point then." As soon as everything was cleared away Celia took the helm, and I stood by at the headsail sheets "All right, run her off for a moment or so to get plenty of way on and then put her about." When Celia put the helm down *Transcur* came wildly flapping into the wind. The mainsail flapped and shuddered as if the mast would be shaken loose by the force of the wind and she put her head down into a sea that came rumbling solid on board. The fore deck was lost to view under a frothing mass of water and then the seas swept right across the cabin top and poured into the cockpit. But *Transcur* came nobly into the wind, paid off on the other tack and gathered way again. We looked at each other in relief and Patrick started the pump.

We worked her up against the wind until we came level with the light vessel at ten in the morning and then with a feeling of relief and exhilaration we let the sheet a little free and raced up the Kiel fjord towards Holtenau. *Transcur* sailed as fast as I have ever seen her sail and as the wind freshened even more I had to ease her by taking down the foresail so that she was left with only her triple reefed mainsail and the tiny spitfire jib, balancing halfway along the bowsprit. "We're done if it blows any harder" I said to Celia "we've run out of reefs." But soon we came into the lee of the land and the fjord became smooth so that *Transcur* was able to go at her maximum speed. She covered the distance from the light vessel to the locks at Holtenau in just inside the hour. We swept up into the yacht basin beside the lock, stowed the sails and Celia and Anne and I drank a large glass of schnapps.

The Kiel Canal seemed to have been foreshortened during our stay in the Baltic and we seemed to pass through it more quickly and with less anxiety than on the outward passage, stopping the night in the same basin as before at Rensborg. Early the next afternoon we were back at Brunsbuttel, in time to squeeze into one of the locks just as it was closing and soon we were out in the Elbe again with enough ebb tide to carry us down to Cuxhaven before dark. "Positively no more messing about in this river at night" Celia warned. But there was a north-westerly breeze to help us down the river, the sun shone brightly and we were able to keep a safe distance from the ships. We came up with Cuxhaven at half past seven and found our way into the harbour where a large number of yachts were lying, some stern to the quay and some alongside. We selected a big German ketch and tied up to her. A friendly man who spoke English took our ropes and soon we were all talking to the owner and his party. There was a young couple honey-mooning in a five tonner and when the big ketch went out, Jutta and Berend brought their boat alongside *Transcur*. Berend was an engineer who had spent some time in England and his wife was a teacher—of English among other things—in a German school.

Jutta and Berend seemed to me to be the reverse side of the coin that I had come to think of as the currency of Germany. I had always been persuaded that Germans were to be despised and shunned as a people who had abused the moral values of civilization. But here was this charming, attractive couple to gainsay it. The real damage to my psychological system had been done in the lifeboat and the years that had passed had not, so far, healed it.

On the second day of our drift in the Atlantic the engineer, my most precious friend, had died. Life had left him without fuss or clamour—I only knew that he was dead because his body, pressed close to mine had become cold. White with distress I told it to the captain, and between us we hoisted the engineer over the side. His body slid down into the calm sea, the captain said an impromptu prayer and the lifeboat was rowed away from the spot so that we should be spared the sight of the sharks at their gruesome work. It was all over in half an hour, the cramped men each moved to take up an inch of vacant space and the ordeal with the sun went on as before. We passed through another day, making some slow progress now with a light breeze, but all of us had become dispirited and weak. The water was beginning to run short, the ration cut from two to one measure in the day. Then on the fourth day a column of smoke was sighted on the horizon which slowly grew into the upper works and then the hull of a small ship. We were picked up and restored to civilization to pursue our separate ways.

The experience, not unnaturally, left me with a distrust—even hatred—of Germans and it was not until we met Jutta and Berend in *Transcur* that I was able finally to shake myself free of this feeling. It is now quite clear to me that German brutalities were no worse in degree or in principle, than those we have committed ourselves and which are being committed at this moment in our names, except that there is a self righteousness about our own excesses that the Germans never had. The gas chambers were no greater a scar on the world than Hiroshima, the bombing of London or my own paltry experience no worse than the destruction of Dresden, and the pogroms of Poland no more disgusting than the current rape of Vietnam. I now believe that what we ourselves are capable of is just as unwholesome as any German barbarities. Jutta and Berend showed me that my resentments were no more than relentless brainwashing from an early age.

Patrick made tea for everybody in both boats the next morning

184

and Berend went ashore and bought fresh white rolls for our breakfast. The forecast gave light westerly breezes which would be of little use to us, but all the same, I decided that we should leave when the tide turned at two p.m. and make what progress we could, hoping for a fair wind later. When the tide turned we said good-bye to Jutta and Berend and slipped out into the busy Elbe. The wind soon left us and we drifted and motored down the endless estuary until finally we saw the light vessel at the entrance shimmering in the refraction. It was now a flat calm, the sea quite smooth with a steady swell heaving up and down and a strong tide carrying us slowly out to sea. It seemed pointless to go on motoring and to use up all our meagre supply of petrol when we still had over four hundred miles to go. We drifted aimlessly, sitting in the sun and playing with the children as *Transcur* described small circles at the mercy of any whim of current, the sails quite lifeless and the smoke from my pipe rising vertically into the torpid air. Then Celia saw an object on the water far away to the northward. I thought it was the hull of a wreck lying on some half submerged sandbank. Celia said it was a stranded whale, Anne thought it was a giant German cigar and Patrick and Adrian both thought it was an island. They were right. The chart showed that it was the island of Heligoland. For a long time we all looked at it and then Anne said "It would be nice to go there". Celia said "Why not, we're not doing any good out here."

It was getting dark when we got near the island and into a well marked approach channel. Suddenly lights began to go on ashore. One by one they spread themselves out round the perimeter of the harbour until within ten minutes there was a blaze of light over what was obviously a fair sized town. By half past nine we were tied up alongside a German yacht in a large safe and busy harbour. "Here we stay until we get a decent breeze" I said to Celia.

Chapter Seventeen

We were tied up alongside a yacht which was in turn tied to a ship of about three thousand tons—we guessed it was some sort of naval depot ship. When Celia and I clambered over her to get ashore after we had put the boys to bed, we saw sailors in naval uniform and there was much saluting and words of command. We walked along half a mile of harbour wall, across a piece of waste ground and then onto an esplanade in front of the town, curving round the perimeter of the harbour. There were few people about in the town—occasionally we would see a dim figure disappear up a side street—yet there were row upon row of neat modern houses and flats grouped into blocks built round small courtyards. There were roads, some of them hardly completed and there were hotels, shops, a few bars and everywhere more building in progress. The houses were all alike as if the town were the brain child of a single commanding architect who was himself responsible for the whole affair from top to bottom. We went into a bar where two or three couples were decorously eating and then to another—the Sea-Horse Bar—where we drank some German beer. Questioned about this strange town the barman would only say "No speak English." There seemed to be no reason for the town's existence and no clue as to how it had got there without the North Sea Pilot knowing anything about it.

The whole island of Heligoland is no more than two miles in length and a half mile across. There were only a few fishing boats in the harbour and no sign of any vast industry to give employment to all these people. We decided that the town must have been built to attract thousands of holidaymakers who had for some reason failed to arrive—perhaps it had been a wild miscalculation on the part of some reckless planner. After three or four beers we wandered perplexedly back to *Transcur*.

The next morning we began to see what it was that made the wheels of life go round in Heligoland. Over the harbour wall from our berth was a small bay and in the early morning two big white modern ships, each of between seven and ten thousand tons, had slid in from the sea and dropped anchor. They were discharging hundreds of passengers into launches which sped in a continuous elipse to the shore and then back for more human freight. On the horizon we saw another white ship approaching fast and soon a fourth appeared. When we walked into the town later in the day it was packed with tourists who seemed to be swarming on the island like locusts, stripping the shops and cafés bare, snip snipping with their expensive cameras and sweeping the horizons with their binoculars.

Anne and I found an elderly lady—charming and dignified—in a souvenir shop, who agreed to change some money for us while Celia took the boys to listen enchanted to a brass band on the esplanade. The lady in the shop had been born in Heligoland long before the war and remembered her mother and father's talk about the island when it had been British in the time of Queen Victoria. "That was a happy time for the islanders" she said. In those days the town had been nothing but a small fishing village which, under the easy patronage of the British, had thrived on a brisk smuggling trade. Then it had been given back to Germany in exchange for Zanzibar, in one of those Imperialist deals of the 1880's "Deutschland, Deutschland, uber alles" had been composed on the island, ironically enough while it was under British rule. It had been a German naval base in the first world war, as in the second, when it had been more or less blasted to pieces by the R.A.F. In 1946 all the inhabitants had been evacu-

187

ated, together with our friend in the souvenir shop, and every building left standing on the island had been destroyed. An attempt had even be made to destroy the island itself with explosives. Now the Germans had come back and with supreme efficiency had built a holiday town to which day-trippers and tourists came in thousands, at least, throughout the summer, to smell the heady North Sea air and to buy duty-free tobacco, drinks and trinkets. The white ships came from the big German industrial towns on the Elbe, the Wesser, the Jade and the Eider from all of which the island is more or less equi-distant.

There was still hardly a breath of wind so that we could not reasonably do anything but wander about the island, bathe on the beach and laze in the sun. Beach bathing seemed to be discouraged by the authorities, presumably to foster trade for an expensive swimming pool where Nordic he-men dived elegantly from a high board and blonde beauties sunned themselves on a tiled terrace in topless bathing suits. On the beach there was a Life Guard, or an official of some sort, who harried us from place to place whenever we tried to swim. When Adrian put on his swimming trunks and ran straight out into the sea, as he always does, the Life Guard came down the beach at a run. "No no do not swim here. Go to the bathing pool." "Why should we not swim here? We like it better in the sea" I asked. He hesitated for a moment and looked at us hard and straight. He wasn't more than twenty years old, with good physique and an open, frank face although not a markedly intelligent one. "Because the English Air Force came here and dropped mines all round the coast" he said with great bitterness, and then turned and walked up the beach.

We found the people on this island were decidedly split into those who liked the English and those who obviously did not. The officers and men of the depot ship which we were lying alongside did not. They made petty regulations about where we might or might not walk across the deck to get to and from *Transcur* and they were hostile towards us, talked and laughed about us behind our backs and were not even friendly towards the children who can usually be relied on to melt the hardest of hearts. There was a resentment—not entirely surprising—which you could have cut with a knife. Ashore, we met a young man in a bar who made no secret of his feelings. "Every other nation in Europe has forgotten about the war", he said "and we're welcomed as friends. But the English keep a grudge longer than anyone else. They still treat us as guilty people." This young man had pale feelingless eyes, an expression of terrifying haughtiness and his face was disfigured with recent duelling scars. He spoke to us in in good English but with a sneer in his voice and he seemed to be devoid of kindliness, sympathy or humour. "That is really frightening" Anne said "I don't mind if we give this bar a miss from now on."

The girl who ran the petrol station near the quay also spoke fluent English. She was at once sympathetic and friendly and nothing that she could do to help us was too much trouble. She loaned us cans to carry our petrol back to *Transcur* and a trolley to carry the heavy tins on board. She refused to accept payment until all our petrol was on board and then she charged us a cheaper rate than was commonly charged on the island—the rate for fishermen. She wanted to know all about our adventures and advised us to shift our berth away from the depot ship and to lie on the other side of the harbour where she pointed out a yacht which she knew, and which she was sure would be friendly towards us. "I hope you will get back to England safely", she said "but the weather is no good for you" and she cocked a knowing eye towards the sky to the westward. In fact, after a still and sunny day the glass was falling and black clouds were coming up from the west. By midnight it was blowing a gale and we spent a restless night tending *Transcur*'s warps and fenders so that she didn't smash herself to pieces alongside the depot ship.

By Monday morning we could not have shifted across the harbour even if we had really wanted to because it was blowing force eight from the west. A flotilla of German M.T.B's came in to shelter in the morning and Dutch and German fishing trawlers entered the harbour one by one throughout the day and tied alongside the quay, thankful to be out of the gale. *Transcur* was now lying next to the depot ship and two German yachts were

189

tied up outside her. We doubled our lines and put every fender we possessed over the side and she lay reasonably quiet although it was rough even inside the harbour. One of the white tripper ships came in during the morning and we watched her dipping her bows into the great seas and flinging spray at the green passengers who lined the promenade deck. They were a sorry lot when they came ashore clasping their cameras under their shiny plastic coats and wishing they had stayed at home for the day. We ourselves were delighted to be safe in Heligoland tied alongside. If we had kept on from the Elbe, instead of coming to Heligoland, we would have been perhaps a quarter of the way to the Terschelling light vessel and the gale would certainly have driven us all the way back to Heligoland and probably further up towards Denmark. *Transcur* was in no state to ride out a North Sea gale in comfort.

I walked round to the other side of the harbour to see the owner of the yacht the petrol girl had told us about, climbed on board and knocked at the cabin door. He was full of charm and concern for us. "When are you due back in England?" "On Saturday." He shook his head sadly. This was no weather for setting out for England and it might go on blowing from the west for weeks on end at this time of year. He took me on to the quay and introduced me to the chief of the weather station who was also friendly, but who spoke very little English. He shook his head sadly as he showed me his maps and graphs and wind instruments and pointed out to me on his enormous wall-map depression after depression following closely one on top of another and stretching from Heligoland across the North Sea, through the English Channel and out into the Atlantic nearly a thousand miles away. "To go to England in a sail boat? Not possible." He reminded me of Mr. Ogerfoorst. I mumbled something about "Maybe the wind will shift southerly between depressions" and walked slowly back to *Transcur* round the end of the harbour.

It was pouring with rain by now and Celia thought we should all dress up in oilskins and walk to the top of the island. The rain had eased the wind and *Transcur* was lying quietly enough to be left. We all trudged up the path to the top of the island

190

from where we could see the seas crashing majestically against the shore, wearing away at the sandstone rock with inexorable persistence and leaving strange toothy projections sticking out of the sea off shore. It was a spectacular sight from up there and bracing ourselves against the wind we looked down on *Transcur* lying in her corner of the harbour with the curling waves hurling themselves against the wall beside her. Another white ship came in and we watched it roll sickeningly as it turned broadside to the seas to enter the smooth water of the bay. A few stalwarts were walking with us up on top of the island, their shiny transparent plastic coats blown out by the wind. Adrian said "Look Mummy, that man must be quite new. He hasn't been unwrapped yet."

We changed our money at a vastly wealthy bank, feeling small and poor as we offered our last five pounds in exchange for a few marks. The other customers at the bank all seemed to be drawing small fortunes over the counter. We bought the boys a splendid tea with pink ice cream, visited the superb aquarium, and then went back to *Transcur* to spend the evening talking and playing cards. The wind was beginning to ease and the glass to climb slowly upwards. On Tuesday the wind had eased to a moderate westerly and the sun came out. This must be our day of departure if we were to stand a chance of being back by Saturday. It would take us over three days in good conditions which it seemed unlikely that we would get. I decided that if the weather was reasonably calm by the evening and the glass was steady, even if the wind was still westerly we would go. If it went southerly we would be all right and even if it only went to the south-west, which was more likely, we ought to be able to fetch to somewhere on the east coast of England. I walked round the harbour wall and saw the weather man again, who was still gloomy about our prospects and showed me on his chart that there was no hope of a high pressure ridge with its attendant northerly or easterly winds. "In one month—you still here" he said with a smile. We all went ashore and drank beer with the very last of our money after Anne and Celia had bought a few odd things to complete our stores. "We'll have to go to sea now",

191

I said "we're flat broke." As we walked back to *Transcur* past the petrol station the girl ran out to say good-bye to us "I have something for the children" she said and gave Patrick and Adrian each a large slab of chocolate.

At seven o'clock, just as it was getting dark, I tapped on the cabin top to the yacht next to us and asked him to move his ropes as we were going out. "You're going out? But it is nearly dark". "That's right." "But you are going out in the dark? And with the children?" "Yes, to get to England you must go in the dark." He bustled about his ropes muttering and mumbling to himself with incomprehension as we slid away from the depot ship. We waved the crew good-bye but they seemed reluctant to return our salute and shuffled off out of sight. "Not one of our social successes" Celia remarked laconically.

We motored out between the harbour piers and turned to the west down the Heligoland channel. There was a heavy swell over the shallow bank outside the harbour—the aftermath of the gale —and *Transcur* rolled and pitched violently. The swells were very steep and did not run true so that she was standing on her head one minute and rolling her scuppers under the next. Everything came adrift down below and slid drunkenly from side to side, the boys were frightened and Celia was apprehensive. "Are we going to go aground again?" Adrian asked quietly. "No, old chap, we shall be all right when we get clear of the land and into deeper water." As *Transcur* rolled to port the propeller would break surface and the engine would race violently. The children began to feel sick at once and even Celia and Anne felt that the beer they had drunk at lunch time was in deep discord with the rest of their insides. "This is quite appalling" Celia said "Could we not go back and wait until it calms down a bit more?" I was edgy. "For Christ's sake be sensible. It'll calm down as soon as we get clear." The Heligoland bank seemed to go on for ever and *Transcur* rolled and pitched so much that I thought the mast would be shaken out of her. I went gingerly forward, holding tight the whole way, and hoisted the foresail in the hope that it would steady her but there was virtually no wind and the foresail only served to increase the racket as it banged from side

192

to side when she rolled. Then gradually we came through the shallows and the swells became lighter and more even. After an hour's motoring we were clear and I set the course 252 degrees for the Borkum Riff light vessel and streamed the log.

At ten o'clock a great big moon came up over the horizon astern of us and with it a breeze from the south-west. We set sail, turned off the engine and we were able to steer 265 degrees, thirteen degrees to the north of our course. The breeze freshened to force four and *Transcur* came to life and began to move fast across the calm and empty sea. Then the wind began slowly to back round to south by west and we were able to steer better than the course, ten degrees to windward to make up for what we had lost and, if possible get a bit further to the south. Suddenly everything was fine. We were sailing fast across the smooth sea and although we were close hauled we were making good our course at four and a half knots. The magnificent moon lighted us with its soft and kindly iridescence and the phosphorous danced splendidly under the bow. So much for our pessimist at the weather station in Heligoland. The boys were peacefully asleep and Anne was making a cup of cocoa. Soon I would leave her to steer and would go to sleep myself in the lee bunk. At eleven o'clock just as I was going off, we picked up a buoy which showed that we were a couple of miles to the north but making good speed. "Keep her steady as she goes" I said to Anne as I handed over the watch "If the wind allows you can luff, but no more than ten degrees. If it heads and you have to bear away, let me know." I pumped the bilge and then went to sleep at once, knowing that *Transcur* was in the charge of capable hands with a steady head behind them, calm and full of concentration. I knew nothing until Celia's hand rested gently on my shoulder four hours later. The breeze was still with us and still allowing us to point our course and we had made nearly twenty miles by the log while I had been asleep. This was almost too good to last. It would be unbelievable luck if we managed to slip across the North Sea right between two of those depressions that the weather man in Heligoland had been so miserable about. At six in the morning another buoy showed us to be still on course although *Transcur* was sailing just as close to the wind as she would go without losing speed. I wondered whether to set the big headsail but decided that what she would make in extra speed she would lose in leeway. The boys were soon up and after breakfast they converted *Transcur* into a floating playground with their games. They were not allowed in the alleyway but the saloon and the fo'c'sle were theirs to build houses in, and to rig overhead lines with boat lacing on which various articles such as bears and cars were hauled backwards and forwards. Between times they would come into the cockpit to talk to whoever was steering or to look at a passing ship or a buoy or even a bird if it called for comment. At ten o'clock our radio direction finder told us that the Borkum Riff light vessel was on the beam although we were too far to the north for it to be visible.

This was the moment when we should alter five degrees to windward in order to follow the correct course but we manifestly could not do this because we were already sailing as close as we could go. Then, just after taking bearings of the Borkum Riff, the wind fell light and died away to nothing leaving us quite becalmed. "This looks like the end of our good run" I remarked to Celia. "At least we've got sixty odd miles on our way." Celia tapped the glass but it was steady. "Maybe we ought to use some petrol and get further to the southward so that if it does come on to blow westerly again we stand a chance of being able to get in somewhere." The big chart across the wall of the Heligoland weather station was firmly fixed in my mind. "I don't fancy being blown back to Heligoland again. I'll give it half an hour and then start the engine." For half an hour *Transcur* lay motionless on the sea, her sails flaccid and the sun shining brightly down on us. We lowered a rope over the side so that the boys could go over in their life jackets and we all went swimming in the cool clean green water, our own shouting and splashing the only noise to be heard. When we were dressed I went to turn on the petrol and start the engine. "Wait a moment" Celia said, "I think a breeze is coming". Sure enough, out to the south a dark patch on the water was bearing down on us. In five minutes the sails were full and drawing and we were bounding along on our course again. The wind had come back, but a point further to the south so that we could head for the Terschelling light vessel. "This is like a miracle" Anne said, "It's easy to see how people—especially sailors—could believe in them." Soon *Transcur* was doing five knots and with the big headsail set another knot was put on. The distance to go was laid off on the chart. "We'll pick up the Terschelling light at nine o'clock to-night."

The day provided one of the finest sails we have ever had. *Transcur* raced through the water with the big headsail pulling steadily and strongly. She was light on the helm and did not need to be steered—a line round the tiller kept her dead on course for the entire day and we were able to play with the children and have our meals all together in the cabin, taking an occasional look at the compass to see that she was behaving properly and sometimes sitting in the cockpit for the sheer pleasure of watching the log spin off the miles and seeing how cleverly the strains and pulls on her sails and sheets kept her going precisely in the right direction. She never varied more than a degree or so either side of the course and no crack ocean racing helmsman could have steered her better. Now I know that Slocum spoke the truth when he recounted how the *Spray* sailed herself. I have seen his contention that she could look after herself on almost any point of sailing disputed in books and have heard yachtsmen cast doubts on it—but now I know it must have been true. From the drawings in the old mariners' books one can see that the *Spray* was very similar in shape—though she was bigger and her rig was different—to *Transcur*. She had the same long straight keel, the same full forepart, the same clear run aft; these are the qualities that gave her sea kindliness. It is precisely these qualities that modern boats have not, with their deep, pointed keels, fine fore parts and bulbous quarters made so, I suspect, to accommodate their large engines. They won't steer themselves for five minutes without complicated and expensive equipment such as wind vanes or electric pilots. If they are left to themselves they sheer into the wind or, what is worse, take the dangerous notion of running to leeward.

We picked up the Terschelling light at half past eight—half

an hour early on the morning's reckoning. We strained our eyes to windward in the dusk but we could see nothing of the island— only the light revolving steadily round once every ten seconds. It was almost exactly four weeks since we had become intimate with Terschelling and we wondered how it was there now. Desolate, as before, only now it would be calm with only the tide grumbling over the sand and turning the water a dull yellow with its timeless disturbance. An occasional gull would swoop and swerve, playing the invisible currents of air to its own ends. The swirly eddies of the tide would decorate the surface of the water with their ominous ringlets. The moon would soon be up to flood its pale light over that lonely place scoured empty and clean by the wind and the sea. We glanced at the Terschelling light with a slight shudder as if to assure ourselves that now we were well away from that sinister bank, out in the clear with plenty of water under us—friendly, pliable, buoyant water to keep us safe. Our brush with the Terschelling bank had left its mark on each of us in its own way. Celia was more nervous and quicker to see danger than she had been before; Anne, I thought, was slightly readier to question my judgments, Adrian was more apprehensive than he used to be. "Is it a hard bottom here Mummy or is it mud?" he would ask in his quiet voice. Patrick had learnt that his father was not infallible in matters connected with the sea and I myself had come some way towards learning that bravado is no substitute for care and attention to detail. *Transcur* had probably come out of it best of all of us. True, she had a few leaks but these would soon be mended in some familiar Essex yard that understood old smacks. But she had proved her immense strength and she had shown us a nobility of character that none of us would ever forget.

After we got past the Terschelling light the wind died away to a whisper and waves of light fog materialised from nowhere and wrapped us in a cocoon of suspended moisture, the moon shining through it, a dim orb. The midnight forecast was for south-westerly winds, veering west, and rain. This must be the beginning of the next depression which would now blow right in our teeth. We drifted about for an hour and then started the engine, keeping it going on and off for most of the night. When a breeze came we sailed, on whichever tack would keep us closest to our course and between breezes we engined. The mist stayed with us all night; occasionally we heard fog horns and the rhythmical beat of engines, too close for comfort but not close enough to give alarm. In the morning there was no sign of wind and we motored on, toying with the idea of putting into Texel but rejecting it partly because we had no money and partly because if we went in, there would be no possibility of getting home on time. We had become so confident in our engine after its sterling work in the Kiel Canal that now we took it quite for granted. At noon a sextant sight determined our latitude and this combined with our dead reckoning to give us something of a position, although we had steered so many different courses during the night that it was unlikely to be accurate. In the afternoon a light breeze came from the north-east of all places and we joyfully set the big headsail and made good progress for a few hours but the day had been unsatisfactory for sailing with the wind fluking all over the place—never blowing true and constant. We reckoned by the log that we made ninety miles in the day. Thursday night was clear with the same uncertain wind that we had become used to. At midnight the Mini-loop gave us a clear signal from the Outer Gabbard light, about twenty miles distant and fine on the port bow—where it should be.

This was the last night of the passage and I knew that for the last time for many months I would be quite alone with *Transcur*. Soon we would all have to make the formidable re-adjustment back to City life—a process I like less and less every time I have to go through it. Perhaps I can contrive things so that the escapes become longer and longer until life is one vast escape and the realities are stowed away in some remote locker never to be looked at again. Society must be in poor shape, I thought, if it can offer me no better prospect than the opportunity to escape from it—or maybe society is right and it's me that is at odds.

It seemed sad to be going home. We had all settled into the routine, got our metabolisms used to the odd hours of sleep and

197

the children were happy and contented—playing away the day, being read to by Celia and Anne and taking an interest in our progress and in what was going on in the great world of sea outside. Patrick was absorbing the elements of seamanship and navigation through his skin. Already he could be left at the helm for quite long periods without losing concentration. Adrian accepted it all as part of the inevitable order of things. Now, we were going to break it all up for the sake of the commercial jungle.

At noon the Outer Gabbard was on the beam and with the whole flood tide under us we were soon making our way through the off lying sands of the Thames Estuary towards the Sunk light vessel. We got to the Sunk at dusk with the last of the tide and then the breeze came up strong from the south-west giving us a hard beat up the Wallet against the ebb tide. It was eleven o'clock before we rounded Brightlingsea bar buoy and quarter to twelve by the time we dropped the anchor in Brightlingsea Creek, three days and four and a half hours to cover the 330 miles—much better than might have been our lot.

The Customs man came on board after breakfast on Saturday but we could find nothing for him worth an entry on his manifest. I went ashore to telephone and to cash a cheque—back to the old routine—and later we all drank a glass of beer and watched *Transcur* at anchor where she had been so many times before, off Brightlingsea hard. She looked innocent enough lying there, very like the other smacks except for her rig, nothing about her to tell you that she was so staunch an ally in adversity, so constant a friend and so true a love. We all looked at her with deep affection as we raised our glasses. Back on board, it was blowing the expected gale. We close reefed the mainsail, set the small jib and set off for Bradwell with the afternoon's flood tide. How it had happened we shall never be sure but in some way we had dodged the furies which had been put our way and we were safe home once again. Soon we would be scheming and planning for another escape.